HERSHEY'S®
FABULOUS DESSERTS

PUBLICATIONS INTERNATIONAL, LTD.

Copyright © 1992 ❌ Hershey Foods Corporation

All rights reserved.
All recipes developed and tested by the Hershey Kitchens.

This edition published by Publications International, Ltd., 7373 North Cicero
Avenue, Lincolnwood, IL 60646

ISBN: 1-56173-886-7

Pictured on the front cover: Chocolatetown Special Cake (*see page 26*).

First published in the United States.

Manufactured in U.S.A.

8   7   6   5   4   3   2   1

Microwave cooking times given in this book are approximate. Numerous
variables, such as the microwave oven's rated wattage and starting
temperature, shape, amount and depth of the food, can affect cooking
time. Use the cooking times as a guideline and check doneness before
adding more time. Lower wattage ovens may consistently require longer
cooking times.

If you have any questions or comments about the recipes in this book, or
about any of our fine Hershey products, please write us at The Hershey
Kitchens, P.O. Box 815, Hershey, PA 17033-0815, or call us, toll-free, weekdays
9am - 4pm Eastern time, at 1-800-468-1714.

CONTENTS

*F*ABULOUS *D*ESSERTS

What comes to mind when you think about chocolate? Perhaps it's chocolate's irresistibly rich and luxurious flavor. That's why millions of us across the country are devoted chocolate lovers. Milton S. Hershey was devoted to chocolate too. When he made his first milk chocolate bar in 1894, little did he know that Hershey would become "America's Chocolate Authority"™.

Today Hershey offers a rich heritage in fine quality chocolates from HERSHEY'S milk chocolate bars and HERSHEY'S KISSES chocolates to the very best for baking with HERSHEY'S cocoa, chocolate chips and baking chocolate. What better way to enjoy the very best chocolate desserts than with Hershey's!

If you've made a batch of Great American Chocolate Chip Cookies from the recipe found on every bag of HERSHEY'S chocolate chips, or seen a recipe in your favorite magazine, then you're familiar with the kind of work we do in the Hershey Kitchens. For over 30 years, we've been developing new chocolate snacks and desserts for all occasions as well as updating popular classics to fit today's lifestyles.

The *HERSHEY'S Fabulous Desserts* cookbook has been designed for all chocolate-loving cooks. The key ingredient in all our recipes is chocolate, of course, and 100% pure HERSHEY'S, too. The easy-to-follow recipe instructions and special hints throughout will help eliminate

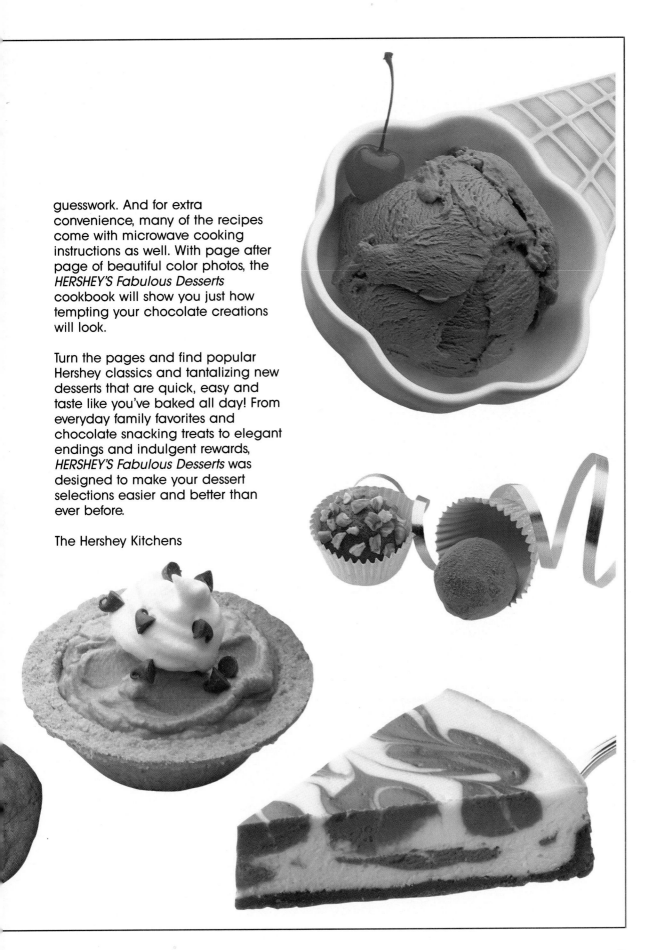

guesswork. And for extra convenience, many of the recipes come with microwave cooking instructions as well. With page after page of beautiful color photos, the *HERSHEY'S Fabulous Desserts* cookbook will show you just how tempting your chocolate creations will look.

Turn the pages and find popular Hershey classics and tantalizing new desserts that are quick, easy and taste like you've baked all day! From everyday family favorites and chocolate snacking treats to elegant endings and indulgent rewards, *HERSHEY'S Fabulous Desserts* was designed to make your dessert selections easier and better than ever before.

The Hershey Kitchens

CAKES & CHEESECAKES

From elegant to easy, indulge yourself with any one of these wonderful cakes.

From left to right: Devil's Delight Cake, Peanut Butter-Fudge Marble Cake (recipes page 8) and Chocolate Sour Cream Cake (recipe page 11)

Devil's Delight Cake

1 package (18.25 ounces) devil's food cake mix (with pudding in the mix)
4 eggs
1 cup water
1/2 cup vegetable oil
1 cup chopped nuts
1 cup miniature marshmallows
1 cup HERSHEY'S Semi-Sweet Chocolate Chips
1/2 cup raisins
    Confectioners' sugar or Chocolate Chip Glaze (recipe follows)

Heat oven to 350°. Grease and flour 12-cup Bundt pan. In large mixer bowl combine cake mix, eggs, water and oil; beat on low speed just until blended. Increase speed to medium; beat 2 minutes. Stir in nuts, marshmallows, chocolate chips and raisins. Pour batter into prepared pan. Bake 45 to 50 minutes or until wooden pick inserted in center comes out clean. Cool 10 minutes; remove from pan to wire rack. Cool completely. Sprinkle confectioners' sugar over top or drizzle Chocolate Chip Glaze over top.

12 to 16 servings

Chocolate Chip Glaze

In small saucepan combine 2 tablespoons butter or margarine, 2 tablespoons light corn syrup and 2 tablespoons water. Cook over low heat, stirring constantly, until mixture begins to boil. Remove from heat; add 1 cup HERSHEY'S Semi-Sweet Chocolate Chips. Stir until chips are melted and mixture is smooth. Continue stirring until glaze is desired consistency.

About 1 cup glaze

Peanut Butter-Fudge Marble Cake

1 package (18.25 or 19.75 ounces) fudge marble cake mix
3 eggs
1/3 cup plus 2 tablespoons vegetable oil, divided
    Water
1 cup REESE'S Peanut Butter Chips

Heat oven to 350°. Grease and flour two 8- or 9-inch round baking pans. Prepare cake batters according to package directions using eggs, 1/3 cup oil and water. In top of double boiler over hot, not boiling, water melt peanut butter chips with remaining 2 tablespoons oil, stirring constantly. OR, in small microwave-safe bowl place chips and oil. Microwave at HIGH (100%) 45 seconds; stir. (If necessary, microwave at HIGH additional 15 seconds or until melted and smooth when stirred.) Gradually add peanut butter mixture to vanilla batter, blending well. Pour peanut butter batter into prepared pans. Randomly place spoonfuls of chocolate batter on top; swirl as directed on package. Bake 30 to 40 minutes or until wooden pick inserted in center comes out clean. Cool 15 minutes; remove from pans. Cool completely on wire rack; frost as desired. *10 to 12 servings*

Collector's Cocoa Cake

¾ cup butter or margarine
1¾ cups sugar
  2 eggs
  1 teaspoon vanilla extract
  2 cups all-purpose flour
¾ cup HERSHEY'S Cocoa
1¼ teaspoons baking soda
  ½ teaspoon salt
1⅓ cups water
    Peanut Butter Cream Frosting
    (recipe follows)

Heat oven to 350°. Grease and flour two 8- or 9-inch round baking pans. In large mixer bowl cream butter and sugar. Add eggs and vanilla; beat 1 minute at medium speed. Combine flour, cocoa, baking soda and salt; add alternately with water to creamed mixture, beating after each addition. Pour batter into prepared pans. Bake 35 to 40 minutes for 8-inch rounds, 30 to 35 minutes for 9-inch rounds, or until wooden pick inserted in center comes out clean. Cool 10 minutes; remove from pans. Cool completely. Frost with Peanut Butter Cream Frosting. Cover; refrigerate frosted cake. *8 to 10 servings*

Creamy Peanut Butter Frosting

  1 package (8 ounces) cream
    cheese, softened
½ cup REESE'S Peanut Butter
¼ cup butter or margarine,
    softened
3⅔ cups (1-pound box)
    confectioners' sugar
  1 teaspoon vanilla extract

In large mixer bowl beat cream cheese, peanut butter and butter until creamy. Gradually add confectioners' sugar and vanilla, beating until well blended.
About 3 cups frosting

Cocoa Cheesecake

Graham Crust (recipe follows)
2 packages (8 ounces each)
cream cheese, softened
3/4 cup plus 2 tablespoons sugar,
divided
1/2 cup HERSHEY'S Cocoa
2 teaspoons vanilla extract,
divided
2 eggs
1 cup dairy sour cream

Prepare Graham Crust; set aside.
Heat oven to 375°. In large mixer
bowl beat cream cheese, 3/4 cup
sugar, cocoa and 1 teaspoon vanilla
until light and fluffy. Add eggs; blend
well. Pour batter into prepared crust.
Bake 20 minutes. Remove from oven;
cool 15 minutes. Increase oven
temperature to 425°. In small bowl
combine sour cream, remaining
2 tablespoons sugar and remaining
1 teaspoon vanilla; stir until smooth.
Spread evenly over baked filling.
Bake 10 minutes. Cool; chill several
hours or overnight.

10 to 12 servings

Graham Crust

In small bowl combine 1 1/2 cups
graham cracker crumbs, 1/3 cup
sugar and 1/3 cup melted butter or
margarine. Press mixture onto bottom
and halfway up side of 9-inch
springform pan.

Chocolate Lover's Cheesecake:
Prepare as above, adding 1 cup
HERSHEY'S Semi-Sweet Chocolate
Chips after eggs have been blended
into mixture. Bake and serve as
directed.

Chocolate Sour Cream Cake

1 3/4 cups all-purpose flour
1 3/4 cups sugar
3/4 cup HERSHEY'S Cocoa
1 1/2 teaspoons baking soda
1 teaspoon salt
2/3 cup butter or margarine,
softened
2 cups dairy sour cream
2 eggs
1 teaspoon vanilla extract
Fudge Frosting (recipe follows)

Heat oven to 350°. Grease and flour
13 x 9 x 2-inch baking pan. In large
mixer bowl combine flour, sugar,
cocoa, baking soda and salt. Blend
in butter, sour cream, eggs and
vanilla. Beat 3 minutes on medium
speed. Pour batter into prepared
pan. Bake 40 to 45 minutes or until
wooden pick inserted in center
comes out clean. Cool completely in
pan on wire rack. Frost with Fudge
Frosting.   *12 to 15 servings*

Fudge Frosting

3 tablespoons butter or
margarine
1/3 cup HERSHEY'S Cocoa
1 1/3 cups confectioners' sugar
2 to 3 tablespoons milk
1/2 teaspoon vanilla extract

In small saucepan over low heat
melt butter. Add cocoa; cook, stirring
constantly, just until mixture begins to
boil. Pour mixture into small mixer
bowl; cool completely. To cocoa
mixture, add confectioners' sugar
alternately with milk, beating to
spreading consistency. Blend in
vanilla.

About 1 cup frosting

Cocoa Cheesecake

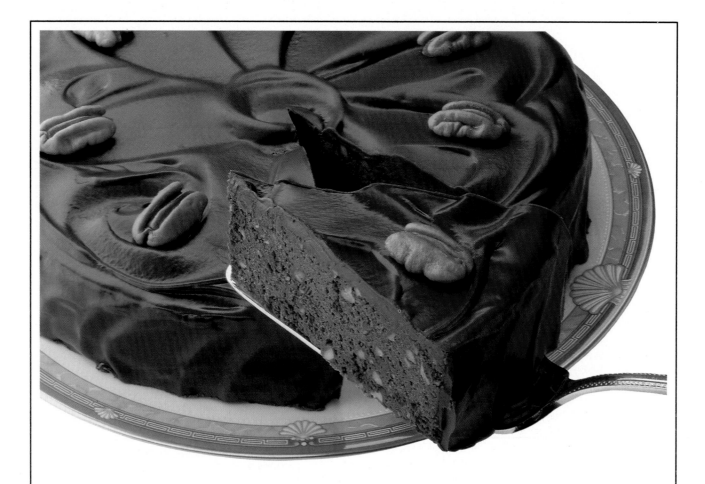

*F*udgey Pecan Cake

   1 cup butter or margarine,
      melted
1¹/₂ cups sugar
1¹/₂ teaspoons vanilla extract
   3 eggs, separated
   ²/₃ cup HERSHEY'S Cocoa
   ¹/₂ cup all-purpose flour
   3 tablespoons water
   ³/₄ cup finely chopped pecans
   ¹/₈ teaspoon cream of tartar
   ¹/₈ teaspoon salt
     Royal Glaze (recipe follows)
     Pecan halves (optional)

Line bottom of 9-inch springform pan with aluminum foil; butter foil and side of pan. Heat oven to 350°. In large mixer bowl combine butter, sugar and vanilla; beat well. Add egg yolks, one at a time, beating well after each addition. Blend in cocoa, flour and water; beat well. Stir in chopped pecans. In small mixer bowl beat egg whites, cream of tartar and salt until stiff peaks form; carefully fold into chocolate mixture. Pour into prepared pan. Bake 45 minutes or until top begins to crack slightly. (Cake will not test done in center.) Cool in pan on wire rack 1 hour. Cover; chill until firm. Remove side of pan. Pour Royal Glaze over cake, allowing glaze to run down side. Spread glaze evenly on top and side. Allow to set. Garnish with pecan halves, if desired.

10 to 12 servings

Royal Glaze

In small saucepan combine 1¹/₃ cups HERSHEY'S Semi-Sweet Chocolate Chips and ¹/₂ cup whipping cream. Cook over low heat, stirring constantly, until chips are melted and mixture begins to thicken.

Jubilee Chocolate Cake

3/4 teaspoon baking soda
1 cup buttermilk or sour milk*
1 1/2 cups cake flour or 1 1/4 cups all-purpose flour
1 1/2 cups sugar, divided
1/2 cup HERSHEY'S Cocoa
1/2 teaspoon salt
1/2 cup vegetable oil
2 eggs, separated
1/2 teaspoon vanilla extract
Vanilla ice cream
Flaming Cherry Sauce (recipe follows)

In medium bowl stir baking soda into buttermilk until dissolved; set aside. Heat oven to 350°. Grease and flour 13 x 9 x 2-inch baking pan. In large mixer bowl combine flour, 1 cup sugar, cocoa and salt. Add oil, buttermilk mixture, egg yolks and vanilla; beat until smooth. In small mixer bowl beat egg whites until foamy; gradually add remaining 1/2 cup sugar, beating until stiff peaks form. Gently fold egg whites into chocolate batter. Pour batter into prepared pan. Bake 30 to 35 minutes or until cake springs back when touched lightly in center. Cool in pan on wire rack. Cut into squares; top each square with scoop of ice cream and serving of Flaming Cherry Sauce.   *10 to 12 servings*

 *To sour milk: Use 1 tablespoon white vinegar plus milk to equal 1 cup.

Flaming Cherry Sauce

1 can (16 or 17 ounces) pitted dark or light sweet cherries, drained (reserve 3/4 cup liquid)
1 1/2 tablespoons sugar
1 tablespoon cornstarch
Dash salt
1/2 teaspoon grated orange peel
1/4 cup kirsch or brandy

In saucepan or chafing dish stir together reserved cherry liquid, sugar, cornstarch and salt. Cook over medium heat, stirring constantly, until mixture boils; boil 1 minute. Add cherries and orange peel; heat thoroughly. In small saucepan over low heat gently heat kirsch or brandy; pour over cherry mixture. Carefully ignite with match. Stir gently; serve as directed. (Repeat procedure for sufficient amount of sauce for entire cake.)

4 to 6 servings

Filled Rich Chocolate Cupcakes

Filling (recipe follows)
3 cups all-purpose flour
2 cups sugar
$2/3$ cup HERSHEY'S Cocoa
2 teaspoons baking soda
1 teaspoon salt
2 cups water
$2/3$ cup vegetable oil
2 tablespoons white vinegar
2 teaspoons vanilla extract

Prepare Filling; set aside. Heat oven to 350°. In large mixer bowl combine flour, sugar, cocoa, baking soda and salt. Add water, oil, vinegar and vanilla; beat on medium speed 2 minutes or until well combined. Fill paper-lined muffin cups ($2^1/2$ inches in diameter) $2/3$ full with batter. Spoon 1 level tablespoon Filling into center of each cupcake. Bake 20 to 25 minutes or until wooden pick inserted in cake portion comes out clean. Remove to wire rack. Cool completely.

About $2^1/2$ dozen cupcakes

Filling

1 package (8 ounces) cream cheese, softened
$1/3$ cup sugar
1 egg
$1/8$ teaspoon salt
1 cup HERSHEY'S Semi-Sweet Chocolate Chips or MINI CHIPS

In small mixer bowl combine cream cheese, sugar, egg and salt; beat until smooth and creamy. Stir in chocolate chips.

VARIATIONS
Goblin's Delight Filling: Add 2 teaspoons grated orange peel, 4 drops yellow food color and 3 drops red food color to Filling before stirring in chips.

Valentine Filling: Add 4 to 5 drops red food color to Filling.

Easy Peanut Butter-Chocolate Chip Cake (left) and Double Marble Cake

Easy Peanut Butter-Chocolate Chip Cake

   1 package (18.5 ounces) yellow cake mix (with pudding in the mix)
   4 eggs
   3/4 cup water
   1/3 cup vegetable oil
   1/3 cup creamy peanut butter
1 1/2 cups HERSHEY'S Semi-Sweet Chocolate Chips, divided
   1/4 cup chopped, unsalted peanuts

Heat oven to 350°. Grease and lightly flour 13 × 9 × 2-inch baking pan. Prepare cake batter according to package directions using eggs, water and oil. Blend in peanut butter. Spoon half of batter into prepared pan. Sprinkle 3/4 cup chocolate chips over batter. Gently spread remaining batter over top. Sprinkle remaining 3/4 cup chips and peanuts over batter. Bake 45 minutes or until wooden pick inserted in center comes out clean. Cool in pan on wire rack.   *12 to 15 servings*

Double Marble Cake

   1 package (18.25 or 19.75 ounces) fudge marble cake mix
   3 eggs
   1/3 cup vegetable oil
       Water
   1 cup HERSHEY'S Semi-Sweet Chocolate Chips, divided
   1 jar (7 ounces) marshmallow creme

Heat oven to 350°. Grease and flour 13 × 9 × 2-inch baking pan. Prepare cake batters according to package directions, using eggs, oil and water. Stir 1/2 cup chocolate chips into chocolate batter. Spoon vanilla and chocolate batters into prepared pan; swirl as directed on package. Bake 33 to 38 minutes or until wooden pick inserted in center comes out clean. Cool in pan on wire rack 5 minutes. Gently spread marshmallow creme over warm cake. In small saucepan over low heat melt remaining 1/2 cup chips; swirl through marshmallow creme. Cool thoroughly.
          12 to 15 servings

Black Forest Torte

Deep Dark Chocolate Cake
(recipe page 18)
1 can (21 ounces) cherry pie
    filling, chilled
1 container (4 ounces) frozen
    whipped topping, thawed

Bake cake in two 9-inch round baking pans as directed. Cool 10 minutes; remove from pans to wire rack. Cool completely. Place one layer on serving plate. Spoon half of pie filling in center and spread to within 1/2 inch of edge. Spoon or pipe border of whipped topping around edge. Top with second layer. Spoon remaining pie filling to within 1/2 inch of edge. Make border around top edge with remaining topping. Chill.   *10 to 12 servings*

Triple Layer Chocolate Mousse Cake

Deep Dark Chocolate Cake
    (recipe page 18)
Chocolate Mousse, Double
    Recipe (recipe page 39)
Sliced almonds (optional)
Chocolate curls (optional)

Bake cake in three 8-inch round baking pans at 350° for 30 to 35 minutes. Cool 10 minutes; remove from pans to wire rack. Cool completely. Prepare Chocolate Mousse, Double Recipe, as directed. Fill and frost layers with mousse. Garnish with sliced almonds and chocolate curls, if desired. Chill at least 1 hour. Cover; refrigerate cake.
          10 to 12 servings

Chocolate Chip Orange Pound Cake

1/2 cup butter, softened
4 ounces (1/2 of 8-ounce
    package) cream cheese,
    softened
3/4 cup granulated sugar
2 eggs
1 teaspoon vanilla extract
1/4 teaspoon grated orange peel
1 cup all-purpose flour
1 teaspoon baking powder
1 cup HERSHEY'S MINI CHIPS Semi-
    Sweet Chocolate
Confectioners' sugar

Heat oven to 325°. Grease and flour 9 x 5 x 3-inch loaf pan. Cut butter and cream cheese into 1-inch slices; place in bowl of food processor. Add granulated sugar; process until smooth, about 30 seconds. Add eggs, vanilla and orange peel; process until blended, about 10 seconds. Add flour and baking powder; process until blended, about 10 seconds. Stir in MINI CHIPS Chocolate. Pour batter into prepared pan. Bake 45 to 50 minutes or until cake pulls away from sides of pan. Cool 10 minutes; remove from pan. Cool completely on wire rack. Sprinkle confectioners' sugar over cake.   *About 10 servings*

Black Forest Torte (top) and Triple Layer Chocolate Mousse Cake

Deep Dark Chocolate Cake

Deep Dark Chocolate Cake

    2 cups sugar
1 3/4 cups all-purpose flour
    3/4 cup HERSHEY'S Cocoa
1 1/2 teaspoons baking powder
1 1/2 teaspoons baking soda
    1 teaspoon salt
    2 eggs
    1 cup milk
    1/2 cup vegetable oil
    2 teaspoons vanilla extract
    1 cup boiling water
    One-Bowl Buttercream Frosting
    (recipe page 26)

Heat oven to 350°. Grease and flour two 9-inch round baking pans or 13 x 9 x 2-inch baking pan. In large mixer bowl combine sugar, flour, cocoa, baking powder, baking soda and salt. Add eggs, milk, oil and vanilla; beat on medium speed 2 minutes. Remove from mixer; stir in boiling water (batter will be thin). Pour into prepared pan(s). Bake 30 to 35 minutes for round pans, 35 to 40 minutes for rectangular pan, or until wooden pick inserted in center comes out clean. Cool 10 minutes; remove from pan(s) to wire rack. Cool completely. (Cake may be left in rectangular pan, if desired.) Frost with One-Bowl Buttercream Frosting.

10 to 12 servings

VARIATION

Chocolate Cupcakes: Prepare Deep Dark Chocolate Cake as directed. Fill paper-lined muffin cups (2 1/2 inches in diameter) 2/3 full with batter. Bake at 350° for 18 to 22 minutes or until wooden pick inserted in center comes out clean. Cool; frost as desired.

About 3 dozen cupcakes

Hot Fudge Pudding Cake

1 1/4 cups granulated sugar, divided
    1 cup all-purpose flour
    7 tablespoons HERSHEY'S Cocoa, divided
    2 teaspoons baking powder
    1/4 teaspoon salt
    1/2 cup milk
    1/3 cup butter or margarine, melted
1 1/2 teaspoons vanilla extract
    1/2 cup packed light brown sugar
1 1/4 cups hot water
    Whipped topping

Heat oven to 350°. In large mixer bowl combine 3/4 cup granulated sugar, flour, 3 tablespoons cocoa, baking powder and salt. Stir in milk, butter and vanilla; beat until smooth. Pour into 8- or 9-inch square baking pan. Combine remaining 1/2 cup granulated sugar, brown sugar and remaining 4 tablespoons cocoa; sprinkle mixture evenly over batter. Pour hot water over top; *do not stir.* Bake 35 to 40 minutes or until center is almost set. Let stand 15 minutes; spoon into dessert dishes, spooning sauce from bottom of pan over top. Garnish with whipped topping.

About 8 servings

*N*o-Bake Chocolate Cheesecake

1 1/2 cups HERSHEY'S Semi-Sweet Chocolate Chips
1 package (8 ounces) cream cheese, softened
1 package (3 ounces) cream cheese, softened
1/2 cup sugar
1/4 cup butter or margarine, softened
2 cups frozen non-dairy whipped topping, thawed
8-inch (6 ounces) packaged graham cracker crumb crust

Microwave Directions: In small microwave-safe bowl place chocolate chips. Microwave at HIGH (100%) 1 to 1 1/2 minutes or until chips are melted and mixture is smooth when stirred. Set aside to cool. In large mixer bowl beat cream cheese, sugar and butter until smooth. On low speed blend in melted chocolate. Fold in whipped topping until blended; spoon into crust. Cover; chill until firm. Garnish as desired. *About 8 servings*

German Chocolate Cake

1/4 cup HERSHEY'S Cocoa
1/2 cup boiling water
1 cup plus 3 tablespoons butter or margarine, softened
2 1/4 cups sugar
1 teaspoon vanilla extract
4 eggs
2 cups all-purpose flour
1 teaspoon baking soda
1/2 teaspoon salt
1 cup buttermilk or sour milk*
Coconut Pecan Frosting (recipe page 21)
Pecan halves (optional)

In small bowl combine cocoa and water; stir until smooth. Set aside to cool. Heat oven to 350°. Grease three 9-inch round baking pans; line bottoms with wax paper. In large mixer bowl cream butter. Add sugar and vanilla; beat until light and fluffy. Add eggs, one at a time, beating well after each addition. Combine flour, baking soda and salt; add alternately with chocolate mixture and buttermilk to creamed mixture. Mix only until smooth. Pour batter into prepared pans. Bake 25 to 30 minutes or until top springs back when touched lightly in center. Cool 5 minutes; remove from pans and peel off paper. Cool completely. Spread Coconut Pecan Frosting between layers and over top. Garnish with pecan halves, if desired. Cover; refrigerate frosted cake.

10 to 12 servings

*To sour milk: Use 1 tablespoon white vinegar plus milk to equal 1 cup.

Coconut Pecan Frosting

1 can (14 ounces) sweetened
    condensed milk
3 egg yolks, beaten
1/2 cup butter or margarine
1 teaspoon vanilla extract
1 can (3 1/2 ounces) flaked
    coconut (about 1 1/3 cups)
1 cup chopped pecans

In heavy 2-quart saucepan combine
sweetened condensed milk, egg
yolks and butter. Cook, stirring
constantly, over medium heat until
mixture is thickened and bubbly,
about 10 minutes. Remove from heat;
stir in vanilla, coconut and pecans.
Cool about 15 minutes.
About 2 3/4 cups frosting

Microwave Chocolate Cake

1/4 cup HERSHEY'S Cocoa
2/3 cup hot water, divided
3/4 cup plus 2 tablespoons all-
    purpose flour
1 cup sugar
1/2 teaspoon baking soda
1/4 teaspoon baking powder
1/4 teaspoon salt
1/4 cup plus 2 tablespoons
    vegetable oil
1 egg
2 teaspoons vanilla extract
    Easy Cocoa Frosting (recipe
    follows)

Microwave Directions: Grease
microwave-safe 7 1/4 x 2 1/4-inch or
8 x 1 1/2-inch round baking dish. Line
bottom of dish with plastic wrap. In
small microwave-safe bowl combine
cocoa and 1/3 cup water; microwave
at HIGH (100%) 40 to 50 seconds or
until very hot and slightly thickened.
In medium bowl combine flour,
sugar, baking soda, baking powder
and salt. Add oil, remaining 1/3 cup
hot water, egg, vanilla and
chocolate mixture; beat with whisk
40 to 50 strokes or until batter is
smooth and well blended. Pour
batter into prepared pan. Microwave
at HIGH 5 to 6 minutes,* without
turning, until cake begins to pull
away from sides (some moist spots
may remain but will disappear on
standing). Let stand 5 minutes; invert
onto serving plate. Peel off plastic
wrap; cool. Frost with Easy Cocoa
Frosting.   *About 8 servings*

*Time is for 600-700 watt microwave
ovens. Increase baking time for lower
wattage ovens.

Easy Cocoa Frosting

3 tablespoons butter or
    margarine, softened
1/4 cup HERSHEY'S Cocoa
1 1/3 cups confectioners' sugar
2 to 3 tablespoons milk
1/2 teaspoon vanilla extract

In small mixer bowl combine all
ingredients; beat to spreading
consistency.   *About 1 cup frosting*

Marbled Angel Cake

1 box (14.5 ounces) angel food
    cake mix
1/4 cup HERSHEY'S Cocoa
    Chocolate Glaze (recipe
    follows)

Adjust oven rack to lowest position. Heat oven to 375°. Prepare cake batter according to package directions. Measure 4 cups batter into separate bowl; gradually fold cocoa into this batter until well blended, being careful not to deflate batter. Alternately pour vanilla and chocolate batters into ungreased 10-inch tube pan. Cut through batter with knife or spatula to marble batter. Bake 30 to 35 minutes or until top crust is firm and looks very dry. Do not underbake. Invert pan on heat-proof funnel or bottle; cool at least 1 1/2 hours. Carefully run knife along side of pan to loosen cake. Place on serving plate; drizzle with Chocolate Glaze.   *12 to 16 servings*

Chocolate Glaze

In small saucepan bring 1/3 cup sugar and 1/4 cup water to full boil, stirring until sugar dissolves. Remove from heat; add 1 cup HERSHEY'S MINI CHIPS Semi-Sweet Chocolate. Stir with wire whisk until chips are melted and mixture is smooth. Cool to desired consistency; use immediately.
About 2/3 cup glaze

Chocolate Cake with Crumb Topping

Crumb Topping (recipe follows)
1 1/2 cups all-purpose flour
1 cup sugar
1/4 cup HERSHEY'S Cocoa
1 teaspoon baking soda
1/2 teaspoon salt
1 cup water
1/4 cup plus 2 tablespoons
    vegetable oil
1 tablespoon white vinegar
1 teaspoon vanilla extract
    Whipped topping or ice cream
    (optional)

Prepare Crumb Topping; set aside. Heat oven to 350°. Grease and flour 9-inch square baking pan. In medium bowl combine flour, sugar, cocoa, baking soda and salt. Add water, oil, vinegar and vanilla; beat with spoon or wire whisk just until batter is smooth and ingredients are well blended. Pour batter into prepared pan. Sprinkle topping over batter. Bake 35 minutes or until wooden pick inserted in center comes out clean. Cool in pan on wire rack. Serve with whipped topping or ice cream, if desired.
About 9 servings

Crumb Topping

In small bowl combine 1/2 cup graham cracker crumbs, 1/4 cup chopped nuts and 2 tablespoons melted butter or margarine. Stir in 1/2 cup HERSHEY'S Semi-Sweet Chocolate Chips.

*Marbled Angel Cake (top) and
Chocolate Cake with Crumb Topping*

All-Chocolate Boston Cream Pie

    1 cup all-purpose flour
    1 cup sugar
    1/3 cup HERSHEY'S Cocoa
    1/2 teaspoon baking soda
    6 tablespoons butter or
        margarine, softened
    1 cup milk
    1 egg
    1 teaspoon vanilla extract
    Chocolate Filling (recipe
        follows)
    Satiny Chocolate Glaze (recipe
        follows)

Heat oven to 350°. Grease and flour 9-inch round baking pan. In large mixer bowl combine flour, sugar, cocoa and baking soda. Add butter, milk, egg and vanilla. Blend on low speed until all ingredients are moistened. Beat on medium speed 2 minutes or until mixture is smooth. Pour into prepared pan. Bake 30 to 35 minutes or until wooden pick inserted in center comes out clean. Cool 10 minutes; remove from pan. Cool completely. Meanwhile, prepare Chocolate Filling. Cut cake horizontally into two thin layers. Spread filling over one cake layer; top with remaining layer. Cover; chill. Pour Satiny Chocolate Glaze on top of cake, allowing some to drizzle down side. Cover; chill several hours. Garnish as desired.   *8 servings*

Chocolate Filling

    1/2 cup sugar
    1/4 cup HERSHEY'S Cocoa
    2 tablespoons cornstarch
    1 1/2 cups light cream or half-and-
        half
    1 tablespoon butter or
        margarine
    1 teaspoon vanilla extract

In medium saucepan combine sugar, cocoa and cornstarch; gradually add light cream. Cook and stir over medium heat until mixture thickens and begins to boil; boil and stir 1 minute. Remove from heat; blend in butter and vanilla. Press plastic wrap directly onto surface. Cool completely.

Satiny Chocolate Glaze

    2 tablespoons butter or
        margarine
    3 tablespoons HERSHEY'S Cocoa
    2 tablespoons water
    1/2 teaspoon vanilla extract
    1 cup confectioners' sugar

In small saucepan over low heat melt butter. Add cocoa and water. Cook, stirring constantly, until mixture thickens; *do not boil*. Remove from heat; add vanilla. Gradually add confectioners' sugar, beating with wire whisk until smooth. Add additional water, 1/2 teaspoon at a time, until desired consistency.
          About 3/4 cup glaze

Marble Cheesecake

    Chocolate Crumb Crust
        (recipe follows)
    3 packages (8 ounces each)
        cream cheese, softened
    1 cup sugar, divided
    1/2 cup dairy sour cream
    2 1/2 teaspoons vanilla extract,
        divided
    3 tablespoons all-purpose flour
    3 eggs
    1/4 cup HERSHEY'S Cocoa
    1 tablespoon vegetable oil

Prepare Chocolate Crumb Crust; set aside. Heat oven to 450°. In large mixer bowl combine cream cheese, 3/4 cup sugar, sour cream and 2 teaspoons vanilla; beat on medium speed until smooth. Gradually add flour; blend well. Add eggs and beat well; set aside. In small bowl combine cocoa and remaining $1/4$ cup sugar. Add oil, remaining $1/2$ teaspoon vanilla and $1 1/2$ cups of cream cheese mixture; blend well. Spoon plain and chocolate mixtures alternately into cooled crust, ending with dollops of chocolate on top. Swirl gently with metal spatula or knife to marble. Bake 10 minutes. Without opening oven door, decrease temperature to 250° and continue to bake 30 minutes. Turn off oven; leave cheesecake in oven 30 minutes without opening door. Remove from oven; loosen cake from side of pan. Cool completely. Cover; chill.   *10 to 12 servings*

Chocolate Crumb Crust

 1 cup vanilla wafer crumbs
    (about 30 wafers)
 $1/4$ cup confectioners' sugar
 $1/4$ cup HERSHEY'S Cocoa
 $1/4$ cup butter or margarine,
    melted

Heat oven to 350°. In medium bowl stir together crumbs, confectioners' sugar and cocoa. Stir in butter. Press mixture onto bottom and $1/2$ inch up side of 9-inch springform pan. Bake 8 minutes; cool.

Marble Cheesecake

Chocolatetown Special Cake

1/2 cup HERSHEY'S Cocoa
1/2 cup boiling water
2/3 cup shortening
1 3/4 cups sugar
1 teaspoon vanilla extract
2 eggs
2 1/4 cups all-purpose flour
1 1/2 teaspoons baking soda
1/2 teaspoon salt
1 1/3 cups buttermilk or sour milk*
One-Bowl Buttercream Frosting
(recipe follows)

In small bowl stir together cocoa and boiling water until smooth; set aside. Heat oven to 350°. Grease and flour two 9-inch round baking pans. In large mixer bowl cream shortening, sugar and vanilla until light and fluffy. Add eggs; beat well. Combine flour, baking soda and salt; add alternately with buttermilk to creamed mixture. Blend in cocoa mixture. Pour into prepared pans. Bake 35 to 40 minutes or until wooden pick inserted in center comes out clean. Cool 10 minutes; remove from pans. Cool completely; frost with One-Bowl Buttercream Frosting. Garnish as desired.

10 to 12 servings

*To sour milk: Use 1 tablespoon plus 1 teaspoon white vinegar plus milk to equal 1 1/3 cups.

One-Bowl Buttercream Frosting

6 tablespoons butter or
  margarine, softened
HERSHEY'S Cocoa:
  1/3 cup for light flavor
  1/2 cup for medium flavor
  3/4 cup for dark flavor
2 2/3 cups confectioners' sugar
1/3 cup milk
1 teaspoon vanilla extract

In small mixer bowl cream butter. Add cocoa and confectioners' sugar alternately with milk; beat to spreading consistency (additional milk may be needed). Blend in vanilla.

About 2 cups frosting

Chocolate Cherry Upside-Down Cake

1 tablespoon cold water
1 tablespoon cornstarch
1/4 to 1/2 teaspoon almond extract (optional)
1 can (21 ounces) cherry pie filling
1²/₃ cups all-purpose flour
1 cup sugar
1/4 cup HERSHEY'S Cocoa
1 teaspoon baking soda
1/2 teaspoon salt
1 cup water
1/3 cup vegetable oil
1 teaspoon white vinegar
1/2 teaspoon vanilla extract

Heat oven to 350°. In medium bowl combine cold water, cornstarch and almond extract, if desired. Stir in cherry pie filling; blend well. Spread evenly on bottom of ungreased 9-inch square baking pan; set aside. In medium bowl combine flour, sugar, cocoa, baking soda and salt. Add water, oil, vinegar and vanilla; beat with spoon or wire whisk until batter is smooth and well blended. Pour evenly over cherries. Bake 40 to 45 minutes or until wooden pick inserted in center comes out clean. Cool 10 minutes; invert onto serving plate. Serve warm.

About 9 servings

Chocolate Stripe Cake

  1 package (about 18.25 ounces)
    white cake mix
  1 envelope unflavored gelatin
  1/4 cup cold water
  1/4 cup boiling water
  1 cup HERSHEY'S Syrup
    Whipped topping

Heat oven to 350°F. Line 13 x 9 x 2-inch baking pan with foil; grease and flour foil. Prepare cake batter and bake according to package directions. Cool 15 minutes; do *not* remove cake from pan. With end of drinking straw, carefully pierce down through cake to bottom of pan, making rows about 1 inch apart covering length and width of cake. In small bowl, sprinkle gelatin over cold water; let stand 1 minute to soften. Add boiling water; stir until gelatin is completely dissolved and mixture is clear. Stir in syrup. Pour chocolate mixture evenly over cooled cake, making sure entire top is covered and mixture has flowed into holes. Cover; refrigerate about 5 hours or until set. Remove cake from pan; peel off foil. Spread with whipped topping. Cover; refrigerate leftovers.

12 to 15 servings

Cocoa Bundt Cake

1 2/3 cups all-purpose flour
1 1/2 cups sugar
  1/2 cup HERSHEY'S Cocoa
1 1/2 teaspoons baking soda
  1 teaspoon salt
  1/2 teaspoon baking powder
  2 eggs
  1/2 cup shortening
1 1/2 cups buttermilk or sour milk*
  1 teaspoon vanilla extract
    Cocoa Glaze (recipe follows)

Heat oven to 350°. Generously grease and flour 12-cup Bundt pan. In large mixer bowl blend flour, sugar, cocoa, baking soda, salt and baking powder; add remaining ingredients except Cocoa Glaze. Beat on low speed 1 minute, scraping bowl constantly. Beat on high speed 3 minutes, scraping bowl occasionally. Pour into prepared pan. Bake 50 to 55 minutes or until wooden pick inserted in center comes out clean. Cool 10 minutes; remove from pan to wire rack. Cool completely. Drizzle with Cocoa Glaze. Garnish as desired.

12 to 16 servings

*To sour milk: Use 1 tablespoon plus 1 1/2 teaspoons white vinegar plus milk to equal 1 1/2 cups.

Cocoa Glaze

  2 tablespoons butter or
    margarine
  2 tablespoons HERSHEY'S Cocoa
  2 tablespoons water
  1 cup confectioners' sugar
  1/2 teaspoon vanilla extract

In small saucepan over low heat melt butter; add cocoa and water, stirring constantly, until mixture thickens. *Do not boil.* Remove from heat; gradually add confectioners' sugar and vanilla, beating with wire whisk until smooth. Add additional water, 1/2 teaspoon at a time, until desired consistency.

About 3/4 cup glaze

VARIATION
Cocoa Sheet Cake: Prepare batter as directed; pour into greased and floured 13 x 9 x 2-inch baking pan. Bake at 350° for 35 to 40 minutes or until wooden pick inserted in center comes out clean. Cool completely; frost with One-Bowl Buttercream Frosting (recipe page 26).

Cocoa Bundt Cake

Cool DESSERTS

Soothing, refreshing desserts for everyday or for entertaining guests.

From left to right: Easy Double Chocolate Ice Cream, Creamy Smooth Choco-Blueberry Parfaits and Chocolate Mint Dessert (recipes page 32)

Chocolate Mint Dessert

  1 cup all-purpose flour
  1 cup sugar
  1/2 cup butter or margarine, softened
  4 eggs
  1 1/2 cups (16-ounce can) HERSHEY'S Syrup
  Mint Cream Center (recipe follows)
  Chocolate Topping (recipe follows)

Heat oven to 350°. Grease 13 x 9 x 2-inch baking pan. In large mixer bowl combine flour, sugar, butter, eggs and syrup; beat until smooth. Pour into prepared pan; bake 25 to 30 minutes or until top springs back when touched lightly. Cool completely in pan. Spread Mint Cream Center on cake; cover and chill. Pour Chocolate Topping over chilled dessert. Cover; chill at least 1 hour before serving. Garnish as desired.   *About 12 servings*

Mint Cream Center

  2 cups confectioners' sugar
  1/2 cup butter or margarine, softened
  2 tablespoons green creme de menthe*

In small mixer bowl combine confectioners' sugar, butter and creme de menthe; beat until smooth.

*1 tablespoon water, 1/2 to 3/4 teaspoon mint extract and 3 drops green food color may be substituted for creme de menthe.

Chocolate Topping

  6 tablespoons butter or margarine
  1 cup HERSHEY'S Semi-Sweet Chocolate Chips

In small saucepan over very low heat melt butter and chocolate chips. Remove from heat; stir until smooth. Cool slightly.

Creamy Smooth Choco-Blueberry Parfaits

  1 package (6 ounces) instant chocolate pudding and pie filling
  2 cups milk
  1/2 cup HERSHEY'S Syrup
  3 1/2 cups (8-ounce container) frozen non-dairy whipped topping, thawed
  1 3/4 cups canned blueberry pie filling, chilled

In large mixer bowl combine pudding mix, milk and syrup; mix well. In separate bowl fold whipped topping into blueberry pie filling; reserve about 1 cup for garnish. Beginning with chocolate mixture, alternately layer with blueberry topping in parfait glasses. Cover and chill. Top with reserved blueberry topping. Garnish as desired.
         6 to 8 parfaits

Easy Double Chocolate Ice Cream

  2 cups chilled whipping cream
  2 tablespoons HERSHEY'S Cocoa
  1 can (14 ounces) sweetened condensed milk
  1/3 cup HERSHEY'S Syrup

Line 9 x 5 x 3-inch loaf pan with foil. In large mixer bowl beat whipping cream and cocoa until stiff. Combine sweetened condensed milk and syrup; fold into whipped cream mixture. Pour into prepared pan. Cover; freeze 6 hours or until firm.   *About 6 servings*

Chocolate Frozen Dessert

1 package (16 ounces)
      chocolate sandwich cookies,
      crushed (about 1³/₄ cups)
¹/₂ cup butter or margarine,
      melted
¹/₂ gallon vanilla ice cream (in
      rectangular block)
      Chocolate Sauce (recipe
      follows)
²/₃ cup pecan pieces (optional)

In medium bowl combine crushed
cookies and butter. Press mixture onto
bottom of 13 × 9 × 2-inch pan or two 8-
inch square pans. Cut ice cream into
¹/₂-inch slices; place over crust.
Cover; freeze 1 to 2 hours or until firm.
Uncover pan(s); pour Chocolate
Sauce over ice cream. Sprinkle
pecan pieces over top, if desired.
Cover; freeze until firm.

About 16 to 18 servings

Chocolate Sauce

2 cups confectioners' sugar
¹/₂ cup butter or margarine
1¹/₂ cups (12-ounce can)
      evaporated milk
1 cup HERSHEY'S Semi-Sweet
      Chocolate Chips

In medium saucepan combine
confectioners' sugar, butter,
evaporated milk and chocolate
chips. Cook over medium heat,
stirring constantly, until mixture boils;
boil and stir 8 minutes. Remove from
heat; cool slightly.

About 2¹/₂ cups sauce

No-Bake Chocolate Cake Roll

1 package (3$\frac{1}{2}$ ounces) instant vanilla pudding and pie filling
3 tablespoons HERSHEY'S Cocoa, divided
1 cup milk
3$\frac{1}{2}$ cups (8-ounce container) frozen non-dairy whipped topping, thawed and divided
1 package (8$\frac{1}{2}$ ounces) crisp chocolate wafers (about 36)

In small mixer bowl combine pudding mix and 2 tablespoons cocoa. Add milk; beat on low speed until smooth and thickened. Fold in 1 cup whipped topping; blend well. Spread about 1 tablespoon pudding mixture onto each chocolate wafer. On foil, stack wafers on edges to form one long roll. Wrap tightly; chill at least 5 hours or overnight. Sift remaining 1 tablespoon cocoa over remaining 2$\frac{1}{2}$ cups whipped topping; blend well. Cover; refrigerate until just before serving. Unwrap roll; place on serving tray. Spread reserved whipped topping mixture over entire roll. To serve, cut diagonally in slices. Store, covered, in refrigerator. Garnish as desired.

About 8 servings

Chocolate-Marshmallow Mousse

1 bar (7 ounces) HERSHEY'S Milk Chocolate Bar
1$\frac{1}{2}$ cups miniature marshmallows
$\frac{1}{3}$ cup milk
1 cup chilled whipping cream

Microwave Directions: Break chocolate bar into pieces; place in medium microwave-safe bowl with marshmallows and milk. Microwave at HIGH (100%) 1 to 1$\frac{1}{2}$ minutes or just until mixture is smooth when stirred; cool to room temperature. In small mixer bowl beat whipping cream until stiff; fold into cooled chocolate mixture. Pour into dessert dishes. Cover; chill 1 to 2 hours or until set.

6 servings

VARIATIONS
Chocolate-Marshmallow Mousse Parfaits: Prepare Chocolate-Marshmallow Mousse according to directions. Alternately spoon mousse and sweetened whipped cream or whipped topping into parfait glasses. Cover; chill about 1 hour.

4 to 6 servings

Chocolate-Marshmallow Mousse Pie: Prepare Microwave Chocolate Crumb Crust (recipe follows) or use 8-inch (6 ounces) packaged chocolate flavored crumb crust. Prepare Chocolate-Marshmallow Mousse according to directions. Pour into crust. Cover; chill 2 to 3 hours or until firm. Garnish as desired.

8 servings

Microwave Chocolate Crumb Crust

Grease microwave-safe 9-inch pie plate. In small microwave-safe bowl place $\frac{1}{2}$ cup butter or margarine. Microwave at HIGH (100%) about 1 minute or until melted. Stir in 1$\frac{1}{2}$ cups graham cracker crumbs, 6 tablespoons HERSHEY'S Cocoa and $\frac{1}{3}$ cup confectioners' sugar until well blended. Press onto bottom and up sides of prepared pie plate. Microwave at HIGH 1 to 1$\frac{1}{2}$ minutes or until blistered; *do not overcook.* Cool completely before filling.

No-Bake Chocolate Cake Roll

Chocolate Butter Pecan Ice Cream

1/2 cup coarsely chopped pecans
1 tablespoon butter
1/2 cup HERSHEY'S Cocoa
2/3 cup water
1 can (14 ounces) sweetened condensed milk
2 teaspoons vanilla extract
2 cups chilled whipping cream

In small skillet over medium heat saute pecans in butter 2 minutes; set aside to cool. In small saucepan combine cocoa and water. Cook over medium heat, stirring constantly, until mixture boils. Remove from heat; stir in sweetened condensed milk and vanilla. Pour into 9-inch square pan; freeze until slushy. In large mixer bowl beat cream until stiff. In small chilled bowl whip chocolate mixture; fold into whipped cream. Stir in pecans. Return to square pan; cover and return to freezer. Freeze until firm, 2 to 3 hours, stirring frequently during first hour.

About 1 1/2 quarts ice cream

Chocolate Butter Pecan Ice Cream

Chocolate Coeur a la Creme with Strawberry Sauce

1/2 cup whipping cream, divided
3 tablespoons HERSHEY'S Cocoa
1 tablespoon butter
1 package (3 ounces) cream cheese, softened
1/2 cup confectioners' sugar
1/2 teaspoon vanilla extract
Strawberry Sauce (recipe follows)

Line two 1/2-cup coeur a la creme molds or two 6-ounce custard cups with double thickness of dampened cheese cloth, extending far enough beyond edges to enclose filling completely. In small saucepan combine 1/4 cup whipping cream, cocoa and butter; cook over low heat, stirring constantly, until smooth. Remove from heat; cool. In small mixer bowl beat cream cheese, confectioners' sugar and vanilla until smooth. Add cocoa mixture, blending well. Beat in remaining 1/4 cup whipping cream. Spoon mixture into prepared molds. Fold cheesecloth over top. Place molds on wire rack set in tray or deep plate. Refrigerate 8 hours or overnight. To serve, pull back cheesecloth and invert each mold onto a chilled dessert plate; carefully remove cheesecloth. Serve with Strawberry Sauce.

8 servings

Strawberry Sauce

1 package (10 ounces) frozen strawberries in lite syrup, thawed
1 tablespoon kirsch (optional)

In food processor or blender container puree strawberries. Strain through fine sieve into small bowl. Stir in kirsch, if desired.

About 1 cup sauce

Peanut Butter Sundae Pie

No-Bake Chocolate Crumb
Crust (recipe follows)
1 quart vanilla ice cream
Peanut Butter Chip Ice Cream
Sauce (recipe follows)

Prepare No-Bake Chocolate Crumb
Crust. Cover; freeze. Place scoops of
ice cream into crust. Cover; freeze
until just before serving. Serve with
Peanut Butter Chip Ice Cream Sauce.

8 servings

No-Bake Chocolate Crumb Crust

In small bowl combine 1 cup
graham cracker crumbs, 1/4 cup
HERSHEY'S Cocoa, 1/4 cup sugar and
1/3 cup melted butter or margarine.
Press mixture onto bottom and up
sides of buttered 9-inch pie plate.

Peanut Butter Chip Ice Cream Sauce

1 cup REESE'S Peanut Butter Chips
1/3 cup evaporated milk
2 tablespoons light corn syrup
1 tablespoon butter or
margarine
1 teaspoon vanilla extract

Microwave Directions: In small
microwave-safe bowl combine
peanut butter chips, evaporated
milk, corn syrup and butter; stir.
Microwave at HIGH (100%) 1 to 1 1/2
minutes or until chips are softened;
stir with whisk until chips are melted
and mixture is smooth. Stir in vanilla.
Cool slightly.

About 3/4 cup sauce

Conventional Directions: In small
saucepan combine all ingredients
except vanilla. Cook over low heat,
stirring constantly, until chips are
melted and mixture is smooth. Stir in
vanilla. Cool slightly.

Chocolate Rum Ice Cream

Chocolate Rum Ice Cream

1 cup sugar
2 tablespoons all-purpose flour
1 cup milk
1 egg, slightly beaten
2 bars (2 ounces) HERSHEY'S
Unsweetened Baking
Chocolate, broken into
pieces
1/2 teaspoon rum extract
2 cups chilled light cream

Microwave Directions: In large
microwave-safe bowl combine sugar
and flour; gradually stir in milk. Blend
in egg and baking chocolate
pieces. Microwave at HIGH (100%) 2
to 2 1/2 minutes, stirring frequently, just
until mixture boils and thickens. Add
rum extract; blend with wire whisk
until mixture is smooth. Chill
thoroughly. Add light cream to
chilled mixture; blend well. Freeze in
2-quart ice cream freezer according
to manufacturer's directions.

About 8 servings

Choco-Berry Frozen Dessert (left) and Cherry-Crowned Cocoa Pudding

Choco-Berry Frozen Dessert

3 packages (3 ounces each)
    cream cheese, softened and
    divided
1 cup HERSHEY'S Syrup
1/2 cup water
4 1/2 cups (about 12 ounces) frozen
    non-dairy whipped topping,
    thawed and divided
3/4 cup pureed strawberries (fresh,
    sweetened OR frozen,
    thawed and drained berries)

Line 9 x 5 x 3-inch loaf pan with foil. In large mixer bowl beat 2 packages cream cheese. Blend in syrup and water; beat until smooth. Fold in 3 cups whipped topping. Spoon half of chocolate mixture into prepared pan; freeze 15 minutes. Chill remaining chocolate mixture. In small mixer bowl beat remaining package cream cheese. Blend in strawberries until smooth. Fold in remaining 1 1/2 cups whipped topping. Spoon strawberry mixture over chocolate layer in pan. Top with chilled chocolate mixture. Cover; freeze several hours or overnight until firm. Unmold about 10 minutes before serving. Peel off foil before slicing.
About 10 servings

Chocolate Mousse

1 teaspoon unflavored gelatin
1 tablespoon cold water
2 tablespoons boiling water
1/2 cup sugar
1/4 cup HERSHEY'S Cocoa
1 cup chilled whipping cream
1 teaspoon vanilla extract

In custard cup sprinkle gelatin over cold water; let stand 1 minute to soften. Add boiling water; stir until gelatin is completely dissolved and mixture is clear. Cool slightly. In small mixer bowl stir together sugar and cocoa; add whipping cream and vanilla. Beat at medium speed, scraping bottom of bowl occasionally, until stiff peaks form; pour in gelatin mixture and beat until well blended. Spoon into serving dishes. Chill about 1/2 hour.

Four 1/2 cup servings

Double Recipe: Use 1 envelope gelatin; double remaining ingredients. Follow directions above; use large mixer bowl.

Cherry-Crowned Cocoa Pudding

1 cup sugar
1/2 cup HERSHEY'S Cocoa
1/3 cup all-purpose biscuit baking mix
2 cups milk
1 cup water
1 can (21 ounces) cherry pie filling, chilled

In medium saucepan combine sugar, cocoa and baking mix. Stir in milk and water. Cook over medium heat, stirring constantly, until mixture comes to full boil; remove from heat. Pour into dessert dishes. Press plastic wrap directly onto surface. Chill several hours or until set. Garnish with cherry pie filling.

6 servings

Fruited Chocolate Sorbet

1 ripe, medium banana
1 1/2 cups orange juice
1/2 cup sugar
1/4 cup HERSHEY'S Cocoa
1 cup chilled whipping cream

Slice banana into blender container. Add orange juice; blend until smooth. Add sugar and cocoa; blend until thoroughly combined. Add whipping cream; blend well. Pour mixture into 9-inch square pan. Freeze until hard around edges. Spoon mixture into large mixer bowl or blender container; blend until smooth. Pour into 1-quart mold. Freeze 4 to 6 hours or until firm. To serve, unmold onto chilled plate; cut into slices.

About 8 servings

Fast Fudge Pots de Creme

1 package (3 1/2 ounces) chocolate pudding and pie filling
2 cups milk
1 cup HERSHEY'S Semi-Sweet Chocolate Chips or MINI CHIPS

In medium saucepan combine pudding mix and milk. Cook over medium heat, stirring constantly, until mixture comes to full boil; remove from heat. Stir in chocolate chips until melted and mixture is smooth. Spoon into 8 creme pots or demitasse cups. Press plastic wrap directly onto surface. Serve slightly warm or chilled. Garnish as desired.

8 servings

Chocolate-Covered Banana Pops

Peel bananas; cut each into thirds. Insert wooden stick into each banana piece; place on wax paper-covered tray. Cover; freeze until firm. In top of double boiler over hot, not boiling, water melt chocolate chips and shortening. Remove bananas from freezer just before dipping. Dip each piece into warm chocolate, covering completely; allow excess to drip off. Immediately roll in peanuts. Cover; return to freezer. Serve frozen.

9 pops

Chocolate Cream Squares

    Chocolate Graham Crust
      (recipe follows)
  1 package (3 ounces) cream
      cheese, softened
 2/3 cup sugar
  1 teaspoon vanilla extract
 1/3 cup HERSHEY'S Cocoa
 1/3 cup milk
  1 container (8 ounces) frozen
      non-dairy whipped topping,
      thawed

Prepare Chocolate Graham Crust; reserve 1/4 cup crumb mixture. Press remaining crumbs onto bottom of 9-inch square pan; set aside. In small mixer bowl beat cream cheese, sugar and vanilla until well blended. Add cocoa alternately with milk, beating until smooth. Gradually fold in whipped topping until well combined. Spoon mixture over crust. Sprinkle reserved crumbs over top. Cover; chill 6 to 8 hours or until set. Cut into squares.   *6 to 9 servings*

Chocolate Graham Crust
In medium bowl, stir together 1 1/4 cups graham cracker crumbs, 1/4 cup HERSHEY'S Cocoa, 1/4 cup sugar and 1/3 cup melted butter or margarine.

Chocolate-Covered Banana Pops

  3 ripe, large bananas
  9 wooden ice cream sticks or
      skewers
  2 cups (12-ounce package)
      HERSHEY'S Semi-Sweet
      Chocolate Chips
  2 tablespoons shortening
1 1/2 cups coarsely chopped
      unsalted, roasted peanuts

Three-In-One Chocolate Pudding & Pie Filling

3/4 cup sugar
1/3 cup HERSHEY'S Cocoa
2 tablespoons cornstarch
2 tablespoons all-purpose flour
1/4 teaspoon salt
2 cups milk
2 egg yolks, slightly beaten
2 tablespoons butter or margarine
1 teaspoon vanilla extract

In medium saucepan combine sugar, cocoa, cornstarch, flour and salt; blend in milk and egg yolks. Cook over medium heat, stirring constantly, until mixture boils; boil and stir 1 minute. Remove from heat; blend in butter and vanilla. Pour into medium bowl or individual serving dishes; press plastic wrap directly onto surface. Cool; chill.

4 servings

Pie: Reduce milk to 1 3/4 cups; cook as directed. Pour hot pudding into 8-inch (6 ounces) packaged graham crumb crust; press plastic wrap onto surface. Chill; top with sweetened whipped cream or whipped topping before serving. *6 servings*

Parfaits: Alternate layers of cold pudding and sweetened whipped cream in parfait glasses.

4 to 6 servings

Microwave Directions: In 2-quart microwave-safe bowl combine sugar, cocoa, cornstarch, flour and salt; blend in milk and egg yolks. Microwave at HIGH (100%) 5 minutes, stirring several times, or until mixture boils. Microwave at HIGH 1 to 2 additional minutes or until mixture is smooth and thickened. Stir in butter and vanilla. Cool as directed above.

PIES

A tantalizing selection of pies— all easy to make, and easy to enjoy.

Chocolate Grasshopper Pie (recipe page 44)

Chocolate Grasshopper Pie

Microwave Chocolate Crumb
Crust (recipe follows) or
8-inch (6 ounces) packaged
chocolate flavored crumb
crust
3 cups miniature marshmallows
1/2 cup milk
1/4 cup HERSHEY'S Cocoa
2 tablespoons white creme de
menthe
2 tablespoons white creme de
cacao
1 cup chilled whipping cream
2 tablespoons confectioners'
sugar

Prepare crust, if desired; set aside. In medium saucepan combine marshmallows, milk and cocoa. Stir constantly over low heat until marshmallows are melted; remove from heat. Stir in creme de menthe and creme de cacao; cool to room temperature. In small mixer bowl beat whipping cream with confectioners' sugar until stiff. Fold in cooled chocolate mixture. Spoon into crust. Cover and freeze several hours or overnight. Garnish as desired.   *6 to 8 servings*

Microwave Chocolate Crumb Crust

Grease microwave-safe 9-inch pie plate. In small microwave-safe bowl place 1/2 cup butter or margarine. Microwave at HIGH (100%) about 1 minute or until melted. Stir in 1 1/2 cups graham cracker crumbs, 6 tablespoons HERSHEY'S Cocoa and 1/3 cup confectioners' sugar until well blended. Press onto bottom and up sides of prepared pie plate. Microwave at HIGH 1 to 1 1/2 minutes or until blistered; *do not overcook.* Cool completely before filling.

Chocolatetown Pie

9-inch unbaked pastry shell
1/2 cup butter or margarine,
softened
2 eggs, beaten
2 teaspoons vanilla extract or
2 tablespoons bourbon
1 cup sugar
1/2 cup all-purpose flour
1 cup HERSHEY'S Semi-Sweet
Chocolate Chips or MINI
CHIPS
1 cup chopped pecans or
walnuts
Festive Whipped Cream
(optional, recipe follows)

Prepare pastry shell; set aside. Heat oven to 350°. In small mixer bowl cream butter; add eggs and vanilla. Combine sugar and flour; add to creamed mixture. Stir in chocolate chips and nuts; pour into unbaked pastry shell. Bake 45 to 50 minutes or until golden. Cool about 1 hour. Serve warm with Festive Whipped Cream, if desired. Garnish as desired.   *8 to 10 servings*

Festive Whipped Cream

1/2 cup chilled whipping cream
2 tablespoons confectioners'
sugar
1/4 teaspoon vanilla extract or
1 teaspoon bourbon

In small mixer bowl combine all ingredients; beat until stiff.
About 1 cup topping

Chocolate Mousse Pie with Rum Cream Topping

Chocolate Mousse (recipe page 39)
8-inch baked pastry shell or 8-inch (6 ounces) packaged chocolate flavored crumb crust
1 cup chilled whipping cream
2 tablespoons confectioners' sugar
2 teaspoons light rum or 1/4 teaspoon rum extract

Prepare Chocolate Mousse. Pour mixture into pastry shell. In small mixer bowl beat cream, confectioners' sugar and rum until stiff. Spread topping over mousse. Cover; chill at least 2 hours. Garnish as desired.   *6 to 8 servings*

Chocolate Cream Pie

1 package (3 ounces) cream cheese, softened
1/2 cup sugar
1 teaspoon vanilla extract
1/3 cup HERSHEY'S Cocoa
1/3 cup milk
1 container (8 ounces) frozen non-dairy whipped topping, thawed
8-inch (6 ounces) packaged graham crumb crust

In small mixer bowl combine cream cheese, sugar and vanilla until blended. Add cocoa alternately with milk, beating until smooth. Gradually fold in whipped topping until well combined. Spoon into crust. Cover; chill 4 to 6 hours or until set.
6 to 8 servings

Chocolate Mousse Pie with Rum Cream Topping

Cocoa Cloud Pie

2 packages (3 ounces each)
cream cheese, softened
1 cup confectioners' sugar
2 teaspoons vanilla extract
1/2 cup HERSHEY'S Cocoa
1/4 cup milk
2 cups chilled whipping cream
8-inch (6 ounces) packaged
crumb crust

In large mixer bowl beat cream cheese, confectioners' sugar and vanilla until well blended. Add cocoa alternately with milk, beating until smooth. Gradually add whipping cream, beating until stiff. Spoon into crust. Cover; chill several hours or overnight. Garnish as desired.   *6 to 8 servings*

Peanut Butter Tarts

1 package (3 1/2 ounces) instant
vanilla pudding and pie
filling
1 1/2 cups milk, divided
1 cup REESE'S Peanut Butter Chips
6 (4-ounce package) single
serve graham crusts
Whipped topping
Fresh fruit

In small mixer bowl blend pudding mix and 1 cup milk; set aside. In top of double boiler over hot, not boiling, water melt peanut butter chips with remaining 1/2 cup milk, stirring constantly to blend. (OR in small microwave-safe bowl place chips and 1/2 cup milk. Microwave at HIGH (100%) 45 seconds; stir. If necessary, microwave at HIGH additional 15 seconds or until melted and smooth when stirred.) Gradually add to

pudding, blending well. Spoon into crusts. Cover; chill until set. Garnish with whipped topping and fruit.
6 servings

Individual Chocolate Cream Pies

1 1/2 ounces (1/2 of 3-ounce
package) cream cheese,
softened
6 tablespoons sugar
1/2 teaspoon vanilla extract
2 1/2 tablespoons HERSHEY'S Cocoa
2 1/2 tablespoons milk
1 cup chilled whipping cream
6 (4-ounce package) single
serve graham crusts
Whipped topping
HERSHEY'S MINI CHIPS Semi-
Sweet Chocolate

In small mixer bowl beat cream cheese, sugar and vanilla until well blended. Add cocoa alternately with milk, beating until smooth. In separate bowl beat whipping cream until stiff; fold into chocolate mixture. Spoon into crusts. Cover; chill until set. Garnish with whipped topping and MINI CHIPS Chocolate.
6 servings

From top to bottom: Cocoa Cloud Pie, Peanut Butter Tarts and Individual Chocolate Cream Pies

Hershey's Syrup Pie

9-inch baked pastry shell
2 egg yolks
1/3 cup cornstarch
1/4 teaspoon salt
1 3/4 cups milk
1 cup HERSHEY'S Syrup
1 teaspoon vanilla extract
Syrup Whipped Topping
  (recipe follows)
Fresh fruit

Microwave Directions: In medium microwave-safe bowl beat egg yolks. Add cornstarch, salt, milk and syrup; blend well. Microwave at MEDIUM-HIGH (70%) 6 to 8 minutes, stirring every 2 minutes with whisk, or until mixture is smooth and very thick. Stir in vanilla. Pour into baked pastry shell. Press plastic wrap directly onto surface; chill several hours or overnight. Garnish with Syrup Whipped Topping and fresh fruit.
6 to 8 servings

Syrup Whipped Topping
In small mixer bowl combine 1 cup chilled whipping cream, 1/2 cup HERSHEY'S Syrup, 2 tablespoons confectioners' sugar and 1/2 teaspoon vanilla extract. Beat just until cream holds definite shape; *do not overbeat.*
About 2 1/4 cups topping

Fudge Brownie Pie

2 eggs
1 cup sugar
1/2 cup butter or margarine, melted
1/2 cup all-purpose flour
1/3 cup HERSHEY'S Cocoa
1/4 teaspoon salt
1 teaspoon vanilla extract
1/2 cup chopped nuts (optional)
Ice Cream
Hot Fudge Sauce (recipe follows)

Heat oven to 350°. Lightly grease 8-inch pie plate. In small mixer bowl beat eggs; blend in sugar and butter. Combine flour, cocoa and salt; add to butter mixture. Stir in vanilla and nuts, if desired. Pour into prepared pie plate. Bake 25 to 30 minutes or until almost set. (Pie will not test done in center.) Cool; cut into wedges. Serve topped with scoop of ice cream and drizzled with Hot Fudge Sauce. *6 to 8 servings*

Hot Fudge Sauce

3/4 cup sugar
1/2 cup HERSHEY'S Cocoa
1/2 cup plus 2 tablespoons (5-ounce can) evaporated milk
1/3 cup light corn syrup
1/3 cup butter or margarine
1 teaspoon vanilla extract

In small saucepan combine sugar and cocoa; blend in evaporated milk and corn syrup. Cook over medium heat, stirring constantly, until mixture boils; boil and stir 1 minute. Remove from heat; stir in butter and vanilla. Serve warm.
About 1 3/4 cups sauce

Microwave Directions: In medium microwave-safe bowl combine all sauce ingredients except butter and vanilla. Microwave at HIGH (100%) 1 to 3 minutes, stirring often, until mixture boils. Stir in butter and vanilla. Cool slightly; serve warm.

Banana Split Pie

Crumb-Nut Crust (recipe follows)
1¼ cups sugar
⅓ cup cornstarch
⅓ cup HERSHEY'S Cocoa
¼ teaspoon salt
2½ cups milk
2 egg yolks, slightly beaten
3 tablespoons butter or margarine
1 teaspoon vanilla extract
2 medium ripe bananas, sliced
Frozen whipped topping, thawed
Chopped peanuts
Additional banana slices
Maraschino cherries

Prepare Crumb-Nut Crust. In medium saucepan stir together sugar, cornstarch, cocoa and salt. Blend milk and egg yolks; gradually stir into sugar mixture. Cook over medium heat, stirring constantly, until mixture thickens and boils. Boil and stir over low heat 3 minutes. Remove from heat, blend in butter and vanilla. Press plastic wrap directly onto filling; cool about 20 minutes. Arrange banana slices over bottom of crust. Pour filling over bananas; press plastic wrap onto filling. Refrigerate 3 to 4 hours. Remove plastic wrap; top pie with dollops of whipped topping. Garnish with chopped peanuts, banana slices and maraschino cherries.   *8 servings*

Crumb-Nut Crust

1¼ cups graham cracker crumbs
⅓ cup butter or margarine, melted
¼ cup finely chopped peanuts

Heat oven to 350°. In medium bowl combine all ingredients; press evenly onto bottom and up sides of 9-inch pie plate. Bake 8 to 10 minutes; cool.

Chocolate Cheese Pie

Chocolate Cheese Pie

1 package (8 ounces) cream
   cheese, softened
1 package (3 ounces) cream
   cheese, softened
3/4 cup sugar
1 teaspoon vanilla extract
1/4 cup HERSHEY'S Cocoa
2 eggs
1/2 cup whipping cream
   8-inch (6 ounces) packaged
     crumb crust
   Cherry pie or peach pie filling

Heat oven to 350°. In large mixer
bowl beat cream cheese, sugar and
vanilla until well blended. Blend in
cocoa, scraping sides of bowl and
beaters frequently. Add eggs; blend
well. Blend in whipping cream. Pour
into crust. Bake 35 to 40 minutes.
(Center will be soft but will set upon
cooling). Cool to room temperature.
Cover; chill several hours or
overnight. Serve with pie filling.
6 to 8 servings

Chocolate Pecan Pie

   9-inch unbaked pastry shell
1 cup sugar
1/3 cup HERSHEY'S Cocoa
3 eggs, slightly beaten
1 cup light corn syrup
1 tablespoon butter or
   margarine, melted
1 teaspoon vanilla extract
1 cup pecan halves
   Whipped topping

Prepare pastry shell; set aside. Heat
oven to 350°. In medium bowl
combine sugar and cocoa. Add
eggs, corn syrup, butter and vanilla;
stir until well blended. Stir in pecans.
Pour into unbaked pastry shell. Bake
60 minutes. Cool completely. Garnish
with whipped topping.   *8 servings*

BREADS, MUFFINS & COFFEECAKES

Let the irresistible aroma of these breads and coffeecakes fill your kitchen.

Chocolate Chip Banana Bread (top) and Cocoa Oatmeal Muffins (recipes page 54)

Cocoa Oatmeal Muffins

1 cup quick-cooking rolled oats
1 cup buttermilk or sour milk*
1/3 cup butter or margarine, softened
1/2 cup packed light brown sugar
1 egg
1 cup all-purpose flour
1/4 cup HERSHEY'S Cocoa
1 teaspoon baking powder
1 teaspoon salt
1/2 teaspoon baking soda
1 cup raisins
1/2 cup chopped walnuts (optional)

Heat oven to 400°. Grease or paper-line muffin cups (2½ inches in diameter). In small bowl stir together oats and buttermilk; let stand 20 minutes. In large bowl beat butter, sugar and egg until fluffy. Stir together flour, cocoa, baking powder, salt and baking soda; add to butter mixture alternately with oats mixture. Stir in raisins and walnuts, if desired. Fill prepared muffin cups 2/3 full with batter. Bake 18 to 20 minutes or until wooden pick inserted in center comes out clean.

About 14 muffins

*To sour milk: Use 1 tablespoon white vinegar plus milk to equal 1 cup.

Chocolate Chip Banana Bread

2 cups all-purpose flour
1 cup sugar
1 teaspoon baking powder
1/2 teaspoon baking soda
1 teaspoon salt
1 cup mashed ripe bananas (about 3 small)
1/2 cup shortening
2 eggs
1 cup HERSHEY'S Semi-Sweet Chocolate Chips
1/2 cup chopped walnuts

Heat oven to 350°. Grease bottoms only of two 8½ x 4½ x 2½-inch loaf pans. In large mixer bowl combine all ingredients except chocolate chips and walnuts; blend well on medium speed. Stir in chips and walnuts. Pour into prepared pans. Bake 45 to 50 minutes or until wooden pick inserted in center comes out clean. Cool 10 minutes; remove from pans. Cool completely on wire rack. *2 loaves*

Chocolate Almond Braided Coffeecake

1/3 cup HERSHEY'S Semi-Sweet Chocolate Chips, melted and cooled
1/3 cup sugar
1/4 cup dairy sour cream
2 tablespoons chopped, toasted almonds*
1 can (8 ounces) refrigerated quick crescent dinner rolls

Heat oven to 350°. In small mixer bowl combine melted chocolate, sugar and sour cream; stir in almonds. On ungreased cookie sheet unroll dough into 2 long rectangles. Overlap long sides to form 13 x 7-inch rectangle; press perforations to seal. Spread chocolate mixture in 2-inch strip lengthwise down center of dough. Make cuts 1 inch apart on each side just to edge of filling. Fold strips at an angle across filling, alternating from side to side. Fold under ends to seal. Bake 20 to 25 minutes or until browned. Cool; cut into slices. Serve warm. *8 servings*

*To toast almonds: Toast in shallow baking pan in 350° oven, stirring occasionally, 8 to 10 minutes or until golden brown.

Chocolate Dessert Waffles

1/2 cup HERSHEY'S Cocoa
1/4 cup butter or margarine, melted
3/4 cup sugar
2 eggs
2 teaspoons vanilla extract
1 cup all-purpose flour
1/2 teaspoon baking soda
1/2 teaspoon salt
1/2 cup buttermilk or sour milk*
1/2 cup chopped nuts (optional)
   Hot Fudge Sauce (recipe page 49)
   Strawberry Dessert Cream (recipe follows)

In small mixer bowl blend cocoa and butter until smooth; stir in sugar. Add eggs and vanilla; beat well. Combine flour, baking soda and salt; add alternately with buttermilk to cocoa mixture. Stir in nuts, if desired. Bake in waffle iron according to manufacturer's directions. Carefully remove waffle from iron. Serve warm with Hot Fudge Sauce and Strawberry Dessert Cream.
About ten 4-inch waffles

*To sour milk: Use 1 1/2 teaspoons white vinegar plus milk to equal 1/2 cup.

Strawberry Dessert Cream
In small mixer bowl beat 1 cup chilled whipping cream until stiff. Fold in 1/3 cup strawberry preserves and 3 drops red food color, if desired. *About 2 cups topping*

Mini Chips Blueberry Bread

2 packages (14.5 ounces each)
  blueberry nut quick bread
  mix
2 eggs, slightly beaten
¾ cup buttermilk or sour milk*
½ cup vegetable oil
1½ cups HERSHEY'S MINI CHIPS
  Semi-Sweet Chocolate
  Mini Chips Glaze (recipe
  follows)

Heat oven to 350°. Grease and flour
12-cup Bundt pan. In large bowl
combine bread mix, eggs, buttermilk
and oil. Beat with spoon 1 minute. Stir
in MINI CHIPS Chocolate. Pour into
prepared pan. Bake 45 to 50 minutes
or until wooden pick inserted in
center comes out clean. Cool 10
minutes; remove from pan. Wrap
tightly in foil. Cool completely. Glaze
with Mini Chips Glaze.   *12 servings*

*To sour milk: Use 2 teaspoons white
vinegar plus milk to equal ¾ cup.

Loaf Version: Prepare half of batter
as directed above using 1 package
blueberry nut quick bread mix, 1
egg, 6 tablespoons buttermilk or sour
milk, ¼ cup vegetable oil and ¾
cup MINI CHIPS Semi-Sweet
Chocolate. Pour batter into greased
and floured 9 × 5 × 3-inch loaf pan.
Bake; cool as directed above.
                              1 loaf

Mini Chips Glaze

In small saucepan bring 2
tablespoons sugar and 2
tablespoons water to boil, stirring
until sugar dissolves. Remove from
heat; add ½ cup HERSHEY'S MINI
CHIPS Semi-Sweet Chocolate. Stir with
wire whisk until chips are melted and
mixture is smooth; use immediately.
                     About ½ cup glaze

Mini Chips Blueberry Breakfast Cake

1 package (14.5 ounces)
  blueberry nut quick bread
  mix
1 cup dairy sour cream
¼ cup water
1 egg
½ cup HERSHEY'S MINI CHIPS Semi-
  Sweet Chocolate
  Topping (recipe follows)

Heat oven to 350°. Grease bottom
only of 9-inch square baking pan. In
medium bowl combine bread mix,
sour cream, water, egg and MINI
CHIPS Chocolate; stir until well
moistened and blended. Spread into
prepared pan. Sprinkle Topping over
batter. Bake 40 to 45 minutes or until
golden brown. Cool; cut into
squares.   *9 servings*

Topping

In small bowl combine ¼ cup all-
purpose flour, ¼ cup sugar and 2
tablespoons softened butter or
margarine until crumbly. Stir in ¼
cup HERSHEY'S MINI CHIPS Semi-Sweet
Chocolate.

*Mini Chips Blueberry Bread (top) and
Mini Chips Blueberry Breakfast Cake*

Mini Chips Surprise Muffins

1 package (16.1 ounces) nut
   quick bread mix
1 egg, slightly beaten
1 cup milk
¼ cup vegetable oil
1 cup HERSHEY'S MINI CHIPS Semi-
   Sweet Chocolate
⅓ cup fruit preserves, any flavor

Heat oven to 400°. Grease or paper-line 18 muffin cups (2½ inches in diameter). In large bowl combine bread mix, egg, milk and oil. Beat with spoon 1 minute. Stir in MINI CHIPS Chocolate. Fill muffin cups ¼ full with batter. Spoon about ½ teaspoon preserves onto center of batter. Fill muffin cups ¾ full with batter. Bake 20 to 22 minutes or until lightly browned. Serve warm.

About 1½ dozen muffins

Mini Chips Surprise Muffins

Easy Chocolate Zucchini Cake

1 package (16.1 ounces) nut
   quick bread mix
½ cup granulated sugar
1 teaspoon ground cinnamon
¾ cup vegetable oil
3 eggs, slightly beaten
1½ cups shredded zucchini
1 cup HERSHEY'S Semi-Sweet
   Chocolate Chips
   Confectioners' sugar (optional)

Heat oven to 350°. Grease and flour 9-inch square baking pan. In large bowl combine bread mix, granulated sugar, cinnamon, oil and eggs; mix until well blended. Stir in zucchini and chocolate chips; pour into prepared pan. Bake 40 to 45 minutes or until wooden pick inserted in center comes out clean. Cool. Sprinkle confectioners' sugar over top, if desired. Cover; refrigerate leftovers.

9 servings

Mini Chips Pancakes

1 carton (16 ounces) frozen
   pancake batter, thawed
½ cup HERSHEY'S MINI CHIPS Semi-
   Sweet Chocolate
   Fruit syrup or pancake syrup

Lightly grease griddle; heat to 375°. In small bowl combine pancake batter and MINI CHIPS Chocolate. Pour about 2 tablespoons batter onto hot griddle. Turn when surface is bubbly; cook until lightly browned. Serve warm with syrup.

About 14 four-inch pancakes

Chocolate Upside Down Coffeecake

³/₄ cup apple jelly
1 package (16 ounces) pound cake mix
1 cup HERSHEY'S Milk Chocolate Chips, divided

Heat oven to 325°. Grease and flour 9-inch square baking pan. Spread jelly evenly onto bottom of prepared pan. Prepare cake batter according to package directions. Stir in ¹/₂ cup milk chocolate chips. Pour batter over jelly layer, spreading gently and evenly. Sprinkle remaining ¹/₂ cup chips over top. Bake 50 to 55 minutes or until cake springs back when touched lightly. Cool 5 minutes in pan; invert onto serving plate. Cool at least 15 minutes; serve warm.

About 9 servings

Cocoa-Nut Bread

2¹/₄ cups all-purpose flour
1¹/₂ cups sugar
¹/₃ cup HERSHEY'S Cocoa
3¹/₂ teaspoons baking powder
1 teaspoon salt
1 egg
1¹/₄ cups milk
¹/₂ cup vegetable oil
1 cup finely chopped nuts

Heat oven to 350°. Grease and flour 9 x 5 x 3-inch loaf pan. In large bowl combine all ingredients except nuts. Beat with spoon 30 seconds; stir in nuts. Pour into prepared pan. Bake 65 to 70 minutes or until wooden pick inserted in center comes out clean. Cool 10 minutes; remove from pan. Wrap tightly in foil. Cool completely.

1 loaf

Mini Chips Cinnamon Crescents

Mini Chips Cinnamon Crescents

1 can (8 ounces) refrigerated quick crescent dinner rolls
Ground cinnamon
¹/₂ cup HERSHEY'S MINI CHIPS Semi-Sweet Chocolate
Confectioners' sugar

Heat oven to 375°. On ungreased cookie sheet unroll dough to form 8 triangles. Lightly sprinkle cinnamon and 1 tablespoon MINI CHIPS Chocolate on top of each. Gently press into dough to adhere. Starting at shortest side of triangle, roll dough to opposite point. Bake 10 to 12 minutes or until golden brown. Sprinkle confectioners' sugar over top. Serve warm. *8 crescents*

CANDIES & SNACKS

Easiest-ever candies for holiday gift giving, plus plenty of great treats for anytime snacking.

Clockwise from far left: Easy Rocky Road, Pastel-Coated Cocoa Bonbons, Easy Double Decker Fudge (recipes page 62) and Coconut Honey Bars (recipe page 64)

Pastel-Coated Cocoa Bonbons

2 packages (3 ounces each)
    cream cheese, softened
2 cups confectioners' sugar
1/2 cup HERSHEY'S Cocoa
2 tablespoons butter, melted
1 teaspoon vanilla extract
    Pastel Coating (recipe follows)

In small mixer bowl beat cream cheese. Add confectioners' sugar, cocoa, butter and vanilla; blend well. Cover; chill several hours or until firm enough to handle. Shape into 1-inch balls; place on wax paper-covered tray. Refrigerate, uncovered, 3 to 4 hours or until dry. Using long fork dip cold centers into very warm Pastel Coating. Quickly remove. Place on wax paper-covered tray; swirl coating on top of bonbon. Refrigerate until firm. Store in airtight container in refrigerator.

2 dozen bonbons

Pastel Coating

6 tablespoons butter
3 cups confectioners' sugar
1/4 cup milk
1 teaspoon vanilla extract
    Red or green food color

Microwave Directions: In medium microwave-safe bowl combine all ingredients except food color. Microwave at HIGH (100%) 1 to 1 1/2 minutes or until smooth when stirred. Tint pastel pink or green with several drops food color.

Easy Rocky Road

2 cups (12-ounce package)
    HERSHEY'S Semi-Sweet
    Chocolate Chips
1/4 cup butter or margarine
2 tablespoons shortening
3 cups miniature marshmallows
1/2 cup coarsely chopped nuts

Microwave Directions: Butter 8-inch square pan. In large microwave-safe bowl place chocolate chips, butter and shortening; microwave at MEDIUM (50%) 5 to 7 minutes or until chips are melted and mixture is smooth when stirred. Add marshmallows and nuts; blend well. Spread evenly into prepared pan. Cover; chill until firm. Cut into 2-inch squares. *16 squares*

Easy Double Decker Fudge

1 cup REESE'S Peanut Butter Chips
1 can (14 ounces) sweetened
    condensed milk, divided
2 tablespoons butter or
    margarine, softened
1 cup HERSHEY'S Semi-Sweet
    Chocolate Chips
1 teaspoon vanilla extract,
    divided

Microwave Directions: Line 9-inch square pan or 9 x 5 x 3-inch loaf pan with foil; lightly butter foil. In medium microwave-safe bowl, place peanut butter chips, 2/3 cup sweetened condensed milk and butter. In second medium microwave-safe bowl, place chocolate chips and remaining sweetened condensed milk. Microwave bowl with peanut butter chips at HIGH (100%) 1 minute or until chips are melted and mixture is smooth when stirred; stir in 1/2 teaspoon vanilla. Immediately pour and spread evenly into prepared pan. Microwave bowl with chocolate chips at HIGH 1 minute or until chips are melted and mixture is smooth when stirred; stir in remaining 1/2 teaspoon vanilla. Immediately pour and spread over peanut butter layer; cool. Cover; refrigerate until firm. Cut into 1-inch squares. Store in airtight container in refrigerator.

About 2 dozen squares

Chocolate-Marshmallow Treats

2 cups (12-ounce package)
   HERSHEY'S Semi-Sweet
   Chocolate Chips
2 tablespoons shortening
12 large marshmallows
1 1/2 cups pecan halves

In top of double boiler over hot, not boiling, water melt chocolate chips and shortening, stirring until smooth. Remove from heat. Set aside; cool mixture to 85°F. Cut marshmallows in half horizontally; place on wax paper and flatten slightly. Set aside. To form base for treats make 24 clusters by arranging pecans on wax paper-covered tray in groups of five, placing flat side of pecan halves down and ends touching in center. Into center of each cluster of pecans spoon 1/2 teaspoon melted chocolate mixture. Use fork to dip marshmallow halves in melted mixture; place one half over each set of pecan clusters, pressing down slightly. Top with pecan half. Cool completely. Store, covered, in refrigerator.   *2 dozen snacks*

Microwave Directions: In 1-quart microwave-safe bowl place chocolate chips and shortening. Microwave at HIGH (100%) 1 1/2 to 2 minutes, stirring once, until chips are melted and mixture is smooth when stirred. Proceed as above.

Chocolate-Marshmallow Treats

Chocolate Dipped Snacks

1/2 cup HERSHEY'S Milk Chocolate
   Chips
1/2 cup HERSHEY'S Semi-Sweet
   Chocolate Chips
1 tablespoon shortening
   Potato chips, cookies, dried
      apricots or miniature pretzels

Microwave Directions: In small microwave-safe bowl place milk chocolate chips, semi-sweet chocolate chips and shortening. Microwave at HIGH (100%) 1 to 1 1/2 minutes or just until chips are melted and mixture is smooth when stirred. Cool slightly. Dip 2/3 of each snack or fruit into chocolate mixture. Shake gently to remove excess chocolate. Place on wax paper-covered tray. Chill, uncovered, about 30 minutes or until chocolate is firm. Store in airtight container in cool, dry place.
About 1/2 cup coating

Fast Chocolate-Pecan Fudge

1/2 cup butter or margarine
3/4 cup HERSHEY'S Cocoa
4 cups confectioners' sugar
1 teaspoon vanilla extract
1/2 cup evaporated milk
1 cup pecan pieces
Pecan halves (optional)

Microwave Directions: Line 8-inch square pan with foil. In medium microwave-safe bowl place butter. Microwave at HIGH (100%) 1 to 1 1/2 minutes or until melted. Add cocoa; stir until smooth. Stir in confectioners' sugar and vanilla; blend well (mixture will be dry and crumbly). Stir in evaporated milk. Microwave at HIGH 1 minute; stir. Microwave additional 1 minute or until mixture is hot. Beat with wooden spoon until smooth; add pecans. Pour into prepared pan. Cool. Cover; chill until firm. Cut into 1-inch squares. Garnish with pecan halves, if desired. Cover; store in refrigerator.

About 4 dozen squares

Coconut Honey Bars

1/3 cup butter or margarine
1/3 cup packed light brown sugar
1/3 cup honey
1/2 teaspoon vanilla extract
2 cups quick-cooking rolled oats
1 1/3 cups flaked coconut
1/2 cup raisins
1 cup REESE'S Peanut Butter Chips

Heat oven to 400°. Line 8-inch square baking pan with foil; grease foil. In large saucepan melt butter; remove from heat. Add remaining ingredients; stir until blended. Press mixture into prepared pan. Bake 15 to 20 minutes or just until golden brown. Cool completely; cut into bars. *About 2 dozen bars*

Mint 'n Chocolate Fudge

1/2 cup butter or margarine
3/4 cup HERSHEY'S Cocoa
4 cups confectioners' sugar
1 teaspoon vanilla extract
1/2 cup evaporated milk
Pastel Mint Topping (recipe follows)

Microwave Directions: Line 8-inch square pan with foil. In medium microwave-safe bowl place butter. Microwave at HIGH (100%) 1 to 1 1/2 minutes or until melted. Add cocoa; stir until smooth. Stir in confectioners' sugar and vanilla; blend well (mixture will be dry and crumbly). Stir in evaporated milk. Microwave at HIGH 1 to 2 minutes or until mixture is hot. Beat with wire whisk until smooth. Immediately pour into prepared pan. Cover; chill until firm. Spread Pastel Mint Topping evenly over fudge; chill until firm. Cut into 1-inch squares. Cover; store in refrigerator.

About 4 dozen squares

Pastel Mint Topping

In small mixer bowl beat 3 tablespoons softened butter or margarine, 1 tablespoon water and 1/8 to 1/4 teaspoon mint extract until blended. Gradually add 1 1/2 cups confectioners' sugar and 2 drops green or red food color. Beat until smooth.

From top to bottom: Cherries 'n Chocolate Fudge (recipe page 67), Fast Chocolate-Pecan Fudge and Mint 'n Chocolate Fudge

Mocha Truffles

1/4 cup whipping cream
3 tablespoons sugar
3 tablespoons butter
1 1/2 teaspoons powdered instant coffee
1/2 cup HERSHEY'S Semi-Sweet Chocolate Chips
1/2 teaspoon vanilla extract
Chopped nuts or HERSHEY'S Semi-Sweet Baking Chocolate, grated

In small saucepan combine whipping cream, sugar, butter and instant coffee; cook over low heat, stirring constantly, just until mixture boils. Remove from heat; immediately add chocolate chips. Stir until chips are melted and mixture is smooth when stirred; add vanilla. Pour into small bowl; chill, stirring occasionally, until mixture begins to set. Cover; chill several hours or overnight to allow mixture to ripen and harden. Form small amounts of mixture into 1/2-inch balls, working quickly to prevent melting; roll in nuts or chocolate. Cover; store in refrigerator. Serve cold.

About 1 1/2 dozen truffles

Chocolate Pralines

1 1/2 cups granulated sugar
1 1/2 cups packed light brown sugar
6 tablespoons HERSHEY'S Cocoa
1 cup light cream
6 tablespoons butter
1 teaspoon vanilla extract
2 cups coarsely broken pecans

Line 2 cookie sheets with wax paper. In heavy 3-quart saucepan combine granulated sugar, brown sugar, cocoa and light cream. Cook over medium heat, stirring constantly, until mixture boils. Reduce heat to low; cook, stirring constantly, to 234°F. (soft-ball stage) or until syrup, when

dropped into very cold water, forms soft ball which flattens when removed from water. (Bulb of candy thermometer should not rest on bottom of saucepan.) Remove from heat. Add butter and vanilla. *Do not stir.* Cool at room temperature to 160°F. Add pecans. Beat with wooden spoon just until mixture begins to thicken, *about 1 to 2 minutes*, but is still glossy. Quickly drop by teaspoonfuls onto prepared cookie sheets. Cool. Store tightly covered or wrap individually in plastic wrap.

About 3 dozen candies

Chocolate Surprise Truffles

1/2 cup unsalted butter, softened
2 1/2 cups confectioners' sugar
1/2 cup HERSHEY'S Cocoa
1/4 cup whipping cream
1 1/2 teaspoons vanilla extract
Centers: After-dinner mints, whole candied cherries, whole almonds, pecan or walnut halves
Coatings: Confectioners' sugar, flaked coconut, chopped nuts

In large mixer bowl cream butter. In separate bowl combine confectioners' sugar and cocoa; add to butter mixture alternately with whipping cream and vanilla, blending well. Chill until firm. Shape small amount of mixture around desired center; roll into 1-inch balls. Drop into desired coating, turning until well covered. Refrigerate until firm. *About 3 dozen truffles*

Variation: Add 1/2 teaspoon rum extract; decrease vanilla to 1 teaspoon.

Cherries 'n Chocolate Fudge

1 can (14 ounces) sweetened
   condensed milk
2 cups (12-ounce package)
   HERSHEY'S Semi-Sweet
   Chocolate Chips
1/2 cup coarsely chopped
   almonds
1/2 cup chopped candied
   cherries
1 teaspoon almond extract
   Candied cherry halves
   (optional)

Line 8-inch square pan with foil. In
medium microwave-safe bowl
combine sweetened condensed milk
and chocolate chips; stir lightly.
Microwave at HIGH (100%) 1 1/2 to 2
minutes or until chips are melted
and mixture is smooth when stirred.
Stir in almonds, chopped cherries
and almond extract. Spread evenly
in prepared pan. Cover; chill until
firm. Cut into 1-inch squares. Garnish
with cherry halves, if desired. Cover;
store in refrigerator.

About 4 dozen squares

Chocolate Dipped Fruit

1 cup HERSHEY'S Semi-Sweet
   Chocolate Chips
1 tablespoon shortening (not
   butter, margarine or oil)
   Assorted fresh fruit, washed
   and chilled

In top of double boiler over hot, not
boiling, water melt chocolate chips
and shortening; stir until smooth.
Allow mixture to cool slightly. Dip fruit
or fruit slices about 2/3 of the way into
chocolate mixture. Shake gently to
remove excess chocolate. Place on
wax paper-covered tray. Chill,
uncovered, about 30 minutes or until
chocolate is firm.

About 1/2 cup coating

Fudge Caramels

Fudge Caramels

2 cups sugar
2/3 cup HERSHEY'S Cocoa
1/8 teaspoon salt
1 cup light corn syrup
1 cup evaporated milk
1/2 cup water
1/4 cup butter or margarine
1 teaspoon vanilla extract

Butter 9-inch square pan; set aside. In
heavy 3-quart saucepan combine
sugar, cocoa, salt and corn syrup;
stir in evaporated milk and water.
Cook over medium heat, stirring
constantly, until mixture boils. Cook,
stirring frequently, to 245°F on a
candy thermometer (firm-ball stage)
or until syrup, when dropped into
very cold water, forms a firm ball that
does not flatten when removed from
water. Remove from heat; stir in butter
and vanilla, blending well. Pour into
prepared pan; cool. With buttered
scissors cut into 1-inch squares. Wrap
individually.

About 6 dozen candies

In large mixer bowl beat cream cheese and milk until fluffy. Add confectioners' sugar, cocoa and vanilla; blend well. Stir in nuts, if desired. Cover; chill several hours or until firm enough to handle. To form centers shape into 1-inch balls. Place on wax paper-covered tray. Refrigerate, uncovered, 3 to 4 hours or until dry. Using long fork, dip cold centers into Peanut Butter coating. (To remove excess coating, slide fork across rim of pan and tap a few times.) Place on wax paper-covered tray; swirl coating on top of bonbon. If coating becomes too thick, reheat over hot water. OR reheat in microwave at HIGH (100%) 30 seconds. Refrigerate, uncovered, 1 hour. Store in airtight container in refrigerator.

About 10 dozen bonbons

Peanut Butter Coating

In top of double boiler over hot, not boiling, water melt 3¹/₃ cups (two 10-ounce packages) REESE'S Peanut Butter Chips and ¹/₄ cup shortening (not butter, margarine or oil), stirring constantly to blend. Set aside; cool slightly.

Microwave Directions: Make centers as directed. In 2-quart microwave-safe bowl place peanut butter chips and shortening. Microwave at HIGH (100%) 1 to 2 minutes, stirring once, or just until chips are melted and mixture is smooth when stirred. Coat and store bonbons as directed.

Peanutty-Cocoa Bonbons

    2 packages (3 ounces each)
        cream cheese, softened
    1 tablespoon milk
    4 cups confectioners' sugar
    ¹/₃ cup HERSHEY'S Cocoa
    1 teaspoon vanilla extract
    1 cup finely chopped nuts
        (optional)
       Peanut Butter Coating (recipe
        follows)

Chocolate Truffles

³/₄ cup butter
³/₄ cup HERSHEY'S Cocoa
1 can (14 ounces) sweetened
    condensed milk
1 tablespoon vanilla extract
    Cocoa or confectioners' sugar

In heavy saucepan over low heat melt butter. Add cocoa; stir until smooth. Blend in sweetened condensed milk; stir constantly until mixture is thick, smooth and glossy, about 4 minutes. Remove from heat; stir in vanilla. Chill 3 to 4 hours or until firm. Shape into 1¹/₄-inch balls; roll in cocoa or confectioners' sugar. Chill until firm, 1 to 2 hours. Store, covered, in refrigerator.

About 2¹/₂ dozen candies

VARIATIONS

Nut Truffles: Add ³/₄ cup coarsely chopped toasted pecans to chocolate mixture when adding vanilla. (To toast pecans: Toast ³/₄ cup pecan halves in shallow baking pan in 350° oven, stirring occasionally, 6 to 8 minutes or until golden brown. Cool.)

Rum Nut Truffles: Decrease vanilla to 1 teaspoon. Stir in 2 to 3 tablespoons rum or 1 teaspoon rum extract and ³/₄ cup coarsely chopped toasted nuts.

Espresso Truffles: Decrease vanilla to 1 teaspoon. Stir in 1¹/₄ teaspoons instant espresso coffee with vanilla. Roll balls in cocoa or chopped nuts.

Nut-Coated Truffles: Roll balls in chopped nuts.

COOKIES & COOKIE BARS

Here's all kinds of cookies to choose from—all made delicious with chocolate.

Five Layer Bars (left) and Cocoa Cherry Drops (recipes page 72)

Cocoa Cherry Drops

1/2 cup plus 2 tablespoons butter
    or margarine
1 cup sugar
1 egg
1 teaspoon vanilla extract
1 1/4 cups all-purpose flour
6 tablespoons HERSHEY'S Cocoa
1/2 teaspoon baking soda
1/2 teaspoon salt
1 cup chopped maraschino
    cherries, well drained
1/2 cup chopped walnuts
    Walnut pieces (optional)

Heat oven to 350°. In large mixer bowl cream butter and sugar. Beat in egg and vanilla. Combine flour, cocoa, baking soda and salt; blend into creamed mixture. Stir in cherries and chopped walnuts. Drop by rounded teaspoonfuls onto ungreased cookie sheet. Press walnut piece into each cookie, if desired. Bake 10 to 12 minutes or until set. Cool slightly; remove from cookie sheet to wire rack. Cool completely.

About 4 dozen cookies

Five Layer Bars

3/4 cup butter or margarine
1 3/4 cups graham cracker crumbs
1/4 cup HERSHEY'S Cocoa
2 tablespoons sugar
1 can (14 ounces) sweetened
    condensed milk
1 cup HERSHEY'S Semi-Sweet
    Chocolate Chips
1 cup raisins or chopped dried
    apricots or miniature
    marshmallows
1 cup chopped nuts

Heat oven to 350°. In 13 x 9 x 2-inch baking pan melt butter in oven. Combine crumbs, cocoa and sugar; sprinkle over butter. Pour sweetened condensed milk evenly over crumbs. Sprinkle chocolate chips and raisins over sweetened condensed milk. Sprinkle nuts on top; press down firmly. Bake 25 to 30 minutes or until lightly browned. Cool completely; cover with aluminum foil. Let stand at room temperature about 8 hours before cutting into bars.

About 3 dozen bars

VARIATION
Golden Bars: Substitute 1 cup REESE'S Peanut Butter Chips for chocolate chips. Sprinkle 1 cup golden raisins or chopped dried apricots over chips. Proceed as above.

Chewy Chocolate Macaroons

1 package (14 ounces) flaked
    coconut (about 5 1/3 cups)
1/2 cup HERSHEY'S Cocoa
1 can (14 ounces) sweetened
    condensed milk
2 teaspoons vanilla extract
    Red candied cherries, halved

Heat oven to 350°. In large bowl thoroughly combine coconut and cocoa; stir in sweetened condensed milk and vanilla. Drop by rounded teaspoonfuls onto generously greased cookie sheet. Press cherry half into each cookie. Bake 8 to 10 minutes or until almost set. Immediately remove from cookie sheet to wire rack. Cool completely. Store loosely covered at room temperature.

About 4 dozen cookies

Buried Cherry Cookies

Chocolate Frosting (recipe
  follows)
1/2 cup butter or margarine
1 cup sugar
1 egg
1 1/2 teaspoons vanilla extract
1 1/2 cups all-purpose flour
1/3 cup HERSHEY'S Cocoa
1/4 teaspoon baking powder
1/4 teaspoon baking soda
1/4 teaspoon salt
1 jar (10 ounces) small
  maraschino cherries
  (about 44)

Prepare Chocolate Frosting; set
aside. Heat oven to 350°. In large
mixer bowl cream butter, sugar, egg
and vanilla until light and fluffy.
Combine flour, cocoa, baking
powder, baking soda and salt;
gradually add to creamed mixture
until well blended. Shape dough into
1-inch balls. Place about 2 inches
apart on ungreased cookie sheet.
Press thumb gently in center of each
cookie. Drain cherries; place one
cherry in center of each cookie.
Bake 10 minutes or until edges are
set; remove from cookie sheet to wire
rack. Spoon scant teaspoonful
frosting over cherry, spreading to
cover cherry.

About 3 1/2 dozen cookies

Chocolate Frosting

2/3 cup sweetened condensed
  milk
1/2 cup HERSHEY'S Semi-Sweet
  Chocolate Chips

In small saucepan combine
sweetened condensed milk and
chocolate chips. Stir constantly over
low heat until chips are melted and
mixture is smooth, about 5 minutes.
Remove from heat; cool thoroughly.

No-Bake Cocoa Haystacks

1 1/2 cups sugar
1/2 cup butter or margarine
1/2 cup milk
1/2 cup HERSHEY'S Cocoa
1 teaspoon vanilla extract
3 1/2 cups quick-cooking rolled oats
1 cup flaked coconut
1/2 cup chopped nuts

In medium saucepan combine sugar, butter, milk and cocoa. Cook over medium heat, stirring constantly, until mixture comes to a full boil; remove from heat. Stir in remaining ingredients. Immediately drop by rounded teaspoonfuls onto wax paper. Cool completely. Store in cool, dry place.

About 4 dozen cookies

Spiced Chip Cookies

1 package (18.25 or 18.5 ounces) spice cake mix
1 cup quick-cooking rolled oats
3/4 cup butter or margarine, softened
2 eggs
2 cups (11.5-ounce package) HERSHEY'S Milk Chocolate Chips
1/2 cup coarsely chopped nuts

Heat oven to 350°. In large mixer bowl combine cake mix, oats, butter and eggs; mix well. Stir in milk chocolate chips and nuts. Drop by rounded teaspoonfuls onto ungreased cookie sheet. Bake 10 to 12 minutes or until very lightly browned. Cool slightly; remove from cookie sheet to wire rack. Cool completely.

About 4 dozen cookies

Cut Out Chocolate Cookies

1/2 cup butter or margarine
3/4 cup sugar
1 egg
1 teaspoon vanilla extract
1 1/2 cups all-purpose flour
1/3 cup HERSHEY'S Cocoa
1/2 teaspoon baking powder
1/2 teaspoon baking soda
1/4 teaspoon salt
Satiny Chocolate Glaze or Vanilla Glaze (recipes follow)

In large mixer bowl cream butter, sugar, egg and vanilla until light and fluffy. Combine flour, cocoa, baking powder, baking soda and salt; add to butter mixture, blending well. Chill dough about 1 hour or until firm enough to roll. Heat oven to 325°. On lightly floured board or between 2 pieces of wax paper, roll small portions of dough to 1/4-inch thickness. Cut into desired shapes with cookie cutters; place on ungreased cookie sheet. Bake 5 to 7 minutes or until no indentation remains when touched. Cool slightly; remove from cookie sheet to wire rack. Cool completely. Frost with Satiny Chocolate Glaze or Vanilla Glaze. *About 3 dozen cookies*

Cut Out Chocolate Cookies

Satiny Chocolate Glaze

2 tablespoons butter or
  margarine
3 tablespoons HERSHEY'S Cocoa
2 tablespoons water
½ teaspoon vanilla extract
1 cup confectioners' sugar

In small saucepan over low heat,
melt butter. Add cocoa and water.
Cook, stirring constantly, until mixture
thickens; *do not boil*. Remove from
heat; add vanilla. Gradually add
confectioners' sugar, beating with
wire whisk until smooth. Add
additional water, ½ teaspoon at a
time, until desired consistency.

About ¾ cup glaze

Vanilla Glaze

3 tablespoons butter or
  margarine
2 cups confectioners' sugar
1 teaspoon vanilla extract
2 to 3 tablespoons milk
2 to 4 drops food color (optional)

In small saucepan over low heat,
melt butter. Remove from heat; blend
in confectioners' sugar and vanilla.
Gradually add milk, beating with
wire whisk until smooth. Blend in food
color, if desired.

About 1 cup glaze

English Toffee Bars

English Toffee Bars

```
    2 cups all-purpose flour
    1 cup packed light brown sugar
1/2 cup butter
    1 cup pecan halves
      Toffee Topping (recipe follows)
    1 cup HERSHEY'S Milk Chocolate
      Chips
```

Heat oven to 350°. In large mixer bowl combine flour, sugar and butter; mix until fine crumbs form. (A few large crumbs may remain.) Press into ungreased 13 x 9 x 2-inch baking pan. Sprinkle pecans over crust. Drizzle Toffee Topping evenly over pecans and crust. Bake 20 to 22 minutes or until topping is bubbly and golden. Remove from oven. Immediately sprinkle chocolate chips over top; press gently onto surface. Cool completely. Cut into bars. *About 3 dozen bars*

Toffee Topping

In small saucepan combine 2/3 cup butter and 1/3 cup packed light brown sugar. Cook over medium heat, stirring constantly, until mixture comes to boil; boil and stir 30 seconds. Use immediately.

Butter Pecan Squares

```
1/2 cup butter, softened
1/2 cup packed light brown sugar
    1 egg
    1 teaspoon vanilla extract
3/4 cup all-purpose flour
    2 cups HERSHEY'S Milk Chocolate
      Chips, divided
3/4 cup chopped pecans, divided
```

Heat oven to 350°. Grease 8- or 9-inch square baking pan. In small mixer bowl cream butter, sugar, egg and vanilla until light and fluffy. Blend in flour. Stir in 1 cup milk chocolate chips and 1/2 cup pecans. Spread into prepared pan. Bake 25 to 30 minutes or until lightly browned. Remove from oven. Immediately sprinkle remaining 1 cup chips over surface. Let stand 5 to 10 minutes or until chips soften; spread evenly. Immediately sprinkle remaining 1/4 cup pecans over top; press gently onto chocolate. Cool completely. Cut into squares. *About 16 squares*

Butter Pecan Squares

Drizzle Topped Brownies

Drizzle Topped Brownies

1¼ cups all-purpose biscuit baking
    mix
1 cup sugar
½ cup HERSHEY'S Cocoa
½ cup butter or margarine,
    melted
2 eggs
1 teaspoon vanilla extract
1 cup HERSHEY'S Semi-Sweet
    Chocolate Chips or MINI
    CHIPS
Quick Vanilla Glaze (recipe
    follows)

Heat oven to 350°. Grease 8- or 9-inch square baking pan. In medium bowl combine baking mix, sugar and cocoa; mix with spoon or fork until thoroughly blended. Add butter, eggs and vanilla, mixing well. Stir in chocolate chips. Spread into prepared pan. Bake 25 to 30 minutes or until wooden pick inserted in center comes out clean. Cool completely. Drizzle Quick Vanilla Glaze over cooled brownies. Cut into bars.   *About 20 brownies*

Quick Vanilla Glaze
In small bowl combine ½ cup confectioners' sugar, 1 tablespoon water and ¼ teaspoon vanilla extract; blend well.

Signature Brownies

1 package (15 ounces) golden
    sugar cookie mix
½ cup HERSHEY'S Cocoa
½ cup HERSHEY'S Syrup
¼ cup butter or margarine,
    melted
1 egg
½ cup coarsely chopped nuts
No-Cook Fudge Frosting
    (recipe follows)

Heat oven to 350°. Grease 8- or 9-inch square baking pan. In medium bowl combine cookie mix (and enclosed flavor packet) and cocoa. Stir in syrup, butter and egg, blending well. Stir in nuts. Spread into prepared pan. Bake 25 to 30 minutes or until wooden pick inserted in center comes out clean. Cool completely. Frost with No-Cook Fudge Frosting. Cut into bars.   *About 20 brownies*

No-Cook Fudge Frosting
In small bowl combine 2 cups confectioners' sugar, ½ cup HERSHEY'S Syrup, ¼ cup HERSHEY'S Cocoa, ¼ cup melted butter or margarine and ½ teaspoon vanilla extract; blend well. Use immediately.

Chocolate Teddy Bears

2/3 cup butter or margarine
  1 cup sugar
  2 teaspoons vanilla extract
  2 eggs
2 1/2 cups all-purpose flour
  1/2 cup HERSHEY'S Cocoa
  1/2 teaspoon baking soda
  1/4 teaspoon salt

In large mixer bowl cream butter, sugar and vanilla until light and fluffy. Add eggs; blend well. Combine flour, cocoa, baking soda and salt; gradually add to creamed mixture, blending thoroughly. Chill until dough is firm enough to handle. Heat oven to 350°.

To shape teddy bears: For each cookie, form a portion of the dough into 1 large ball for body (1 to 1 1/2 inches), 1 medium-size ball for head (3/4 to 1 inch), 4 small balls for arms and legs (1/2 inch), 2 smaller balls for ears, 1 tiny ball for nose and 4 tiny balls for paws (optional). On ungreased cookie sheet flatten large ball slightly for body. Attach medium-size ball for head by overlapping slightly onto body. Place balls for arms, legs and ears, and a tiny ball on head for nose. Arrange other tiny balls atop ends of legs and arms for paws, if desired. With wooden pick, draw eyes and mouth; pierce small hole at top of cookie for use as hanging ornament, if desired. Bake 6 to 8 minutes or until set. Cool 1 minute; remove from cookie sheet to wire rack. Cool completely. Store in covered container. If cookies will be used as ornaments, allow to dry on wire rack at least 6 hours before hanging. Decorate with ribbon or pull ribbon through hole for hanging, if desired. *About 14 cookies*

Peanut Butter Chips and Jelly Bars

1½ cups all-purpose flour
½ cup sugar
¾ teaspoon baking powder
½ cup butter or margarine
1 egg, beaten
¾ cup grape jelly
1 cup REESE'S Peanut Butter Chips, divided

Heat oven to 375°. Grease 9-inch square baking pan. In medium bowl combine flour, sugar and baking powder; cut in butter with pastry blender or fork to form coarse crumbs. Add egg; blend well. Reserve half of mixture; press remaining mixture onto bottom of prepared pan. Spread jelly evenly over crust. Sprinkle ½ cup peanut butter chips over jelly. Combine remaining crumb mixture with remaining ½ cup chips; sprinkle over top. Bake 25 to 30 minutes or until lightly browned. Cool completely. Cut into bars.

About 1½ dozen bars

Chocolate Crinkle Cookies

2 cups sugar
¾ cup vegetable oil
¾ cup HERSHEY'S Cocoa
4 eggs
2 teaspoons vanilla extract
2⅓ cups all-purpose flour
2 teaspoons baking powder
½ teaspoon salt
Confectioners' sugar

In large mixer bowl combine sugar and oil; add cocoa, blending well. Beat in eggs and vanilla. Combine flour, baking powder and salt; add to cocoa mixture, blending well. Cover; chill at least 6 hours. Heat oven to 350°. Shape dough into 1-inch balls; roll in confectioners' sugar. Place 2 inches apart on greased cookie sheet. Bake 12 to 14 minutes or until almost no indentation remains when touched. Remove from cookie sheet to wire rack. Cool completely.

About 4 dozen cookies

Peanut Butter Chips and Jelly Bars

BEVERAGES

Rich cocoas to warm you in winter, plus frothy favorites to cool you off in summer.

From left to right: Irish Cocoa, Cocoa-Banana Shake and Hot Cocoa (recipes page 82)

Irish Cocoa

6 tablespoons sugar
3 tablespoons HERSHEY'S Cocoa
Dash salt
1/4 cup hot water
3 cups milk
6 tablespoons Irish whiskey
1/2 cup chilled whipping cream, whipped

In medium saucepan combine sugar, cocoa and salt; stir in water. Cook over medium heat, stirring constantly, until mixture boils. Boil and stir 2 minutes. Add milk; stir and heat to serving temperature. *Do not boil.* Remove from heat. Pour 1 tablespoon whiskey in each cup or goblet. Fill cup with hot cocoa; stir to blend. Serve hot, topped with whipped cream.
About six 6-ounce servings

Cocoa-Banana Shake

1 ripe, medium banana
1/4 cup HERSHEY'S Cocoa
1/4 cup honey
1/4 cup hot water
2 cups cold milk
1 cup vanilla ice cream

Slice banana into blender container. Add cocoa, honey and water; cover and blend until smooth. Add milk; cover and blend. Add ice cream; cover and blend until smooth. Serve immediately.
About four 8-ounce servings

Hot Cocoa

1/2 cup sugar
1/4 cup HERSHEY'S Cocoa
Dash salt
1/3 cup hot water
4 cups (1 quart) milk
3/4 teaspoon vanilla extract
Sweetened Whipped Cream (optional, recipe page 88)

In medium saucepan combine sugar, cocoa and salt; blend in water. Cook over medium heat, stirring constantly, until mixture boils. Boil and stir 2 minutes. Add milk; stir and heat to serving temperature. *Do not boil.* Remove from heat; add vanilla. Beat with rotary beater or wire whisk until foamy. Serve hot, topped with Sweetened Whipped Cream, if desired.
About six 6-ounce servings

VARIATIONS
Spiced Cocoa: Add 1/8 teaspoon ground cinnamon and 1/8 teaspoon ground nutmeg with vanilla.

Citrus Cocoa: Add 1/2 teaspoon orange extract or 2 to 3 tablespoons orange liqueur with vanilla.

Swiss Mocha: Add 2 to 2 1/2 teaspoons powdered instant coffee with vanilla.

Mint Cocoa: Add 1/2 teaspoon mint extract, or 3 tablespoons crushed hard peppermint candy, or 2 to 3 tablespoons white creme de menthe with vanilla.

Cocoa au Lait: Omit whipped cream. Spoon 2 tablespoons softened vanilla ice cream on top of each cup of cocoa at serving time.

Slim-Trim Cocoa: Omit sugar. Combine cocoa, salt and water; substitute skim milk. Proceed as above. With vanilla, stir in sugar substitute with sweetening equivalence of 1/2 cup sugar.

Microwave Single Serving: In 8-ounce microwave-safe mug, combine 2 heaping teaspoons sugar and 1 heaping teaspoon HERSHEY'S Cocoa. Add 2 teaspoons cold milk; stir until smooth. Fill mug with milk; microwave at HIGH (100%) 1 to 1 1/2 minutes or just until hot. Stir to blend before serving.

Chocolate Strawberry Cooler

1/2 cup sliced strawberries
2 tablespoons sugar
1 tablespoon HERSHEY'S Cocoa
1 cup milk, divided
1/2 cup cold club soda, freshly opened
Ice cream or whipped cream
2 fresh strawberries (optional)

In blender container combine sliced strawberries, sugar, cocoa and 1/2 cup milk; cover and blend until smooth. Add remaining 1/2 cup milk and club soda; cover and blend. Pour into 2 glasses. Garnish with ice cream or whipped cream and strawberry, if desired. Serve immediately.

About two 8-ounce servings

Chocolate Strawberry Cooler

Double Chocolate Malt

1/2 cup cold milk
1/4 cup HERSHEY'S Syrup
2 tablespoons chocolate malted
    milk powder
2 cups vanilla ice cream,
    softened

In blender container place milk,
syrup and malted milk powder.
Cover; blend. Add ice cream. Cover;
blend until smooth. Serve
immediately.
About three 6-ounce servings

VARIATION
Triple Chocolate Malt: Substitute
chocolate ice cream for vanilla ice
cream.

Hot Cocoa For A Crowd

1 1/2 cups sugar
1 1/4 cups HERSHEY'S Cocoa
1/2 teaspoon salt
3/4 cup hot water
4 quarts (1 gallon) milk
1 tablespoon vanilla extract

In 6-quart saucepan combine sugar,
cocoa and salt; gradually add hot
water. Cook over medium heat,
stirring constantly, until mixture boils.
Boil and stir 2 minutes. Add milk;
heat to serving temperature, stirring
occasionally. *Do not boil.* Remove
from heat; add vanilla. Serve hot.
About twenty-two 6-ounce servings

Hot Merry Mocha

6 tablespoons HERSHEY'S Cocoa
1 to 2 tablespoons powdered
    instant coffee
1/8 teaspoon salt
6 cups hot water
1 can (14 ounces) sweetened
    condensed milk
    Sweetened Whipped Cream
    (optional, recipe page 88)

In 4-quart saucepan combine
cocoa, instant coffee and salt; stir in
water. Cook over medium heat,
stirring occasionally, until mixture
boils. Stir in sweetened condensed
milk; heat thoroughly. *Do not boil.*
Beat with rotary beater or wire whisk
until foamy. Serve hot, topped with
Sweetened Whipped Cream, if
desired.
About ten 6-ounce servings

VARIATION
Minted Hot Chocolate: Follow
directions above omitting instant
coffee. Stir in 1/4 to 1/2 teaspoon mint
extract before beating. Serve with
candy cane for stirrer, if desired.

Cappuccino Cooler

1 1/2 cups cold coffee
1 1/2 cups chocolate ice cream
1/4 cup HERSHEY'S Syrup
    Crushed ice
    Whipped cream

In blender container place coffee,
ice cream and syrup. Cover; blend
until smooth. Serve immediately over
crushed ice. Garnish with whipped
cream.
About four 6-ounce servings

Hot Cocoa Mix

2 cups nonfat dry milk powder
3/4 cup sugar
1/2 cup HERSHEY'S Cocoa
1/2 cup powdered non-dairy
    creamer
Dash salt

In large bowl combine all ingredients; blend well. Store mix in tightly covered container.

3³/4 cups mix
(about fifteen 6-ounce servings)

Single serving: Place ¹/4 cup mix in heatproof cup or mug; stir in ³/4 cup boiling water. Serve hot, topped with marshmallows, if desired.

Choco Peanut Butter Shake

³/4 cup cold milk
¹/4 cup creamy peanut butter
3 tablespoons HERSHEY'S Cocoa
1 tablespoon marshmallow
    creme
2 cups vanilla ice cream

In blender container place milk, peanut butter, cocoa and marshmallow creme. Cover; blend. Add ice cream. Cover; blend until smooth. Serve immediately.

About three 6-ounce servings

Spiced Mocha (from mix)

Spiced Mocha Mix

1 cup sugar
1 cup nonfat dry milk powder
¹/2 cup powdered non-dairy
    creamer
¹/2 cup HERSHEY'S Cocoa
3 tablespoons powdered instant
    coffee
¹/2 teaspoon ground allspice
¹/4 teaspoon ground cinnamon
Dash salt

In large bowl combine all ingredients. Store in airtight container.

2¹/2 cups mix (12 to 14 servings)

For Single Serving: Place 3 tablespoons mix in mug or cup; add ³/4 cup boiling water. Stir until mix is dissolved. Top with marshmallows, if desired. Serve immediately.

EXTRAS

Delicious sauces and frostings plus the luscious dessert recipes pictured on the front cover.

From left to right: Fudge Frosting, Quick Hot Fudge Sauce and Chocolate Whipped Cream (recipes page 88)

Fudge Frosting

1 cup sugar
1/4 cup HERSHEY'S Cocoa
1/2 cup milk
1/4 cup butter or margarine
2 tablespoons light corn syrup
Dash salt
1 1/2 cups confectioners' sugar
1 teaspoon vanilla extract

In medium saucepan combine sugar and cocoa. Stir in milk, butter, corn syrup and salt. Cook over medium heat, stirring constantly, until mixture comes to a full boil. Boil, stirring occasionally, 3 minutes. Remove from heat; cool to lukewarm. In small mixer bowl place confectioners' sugar; stir in chocolate mixture and vanilla. Beat until spreading consistency.

About 2 cups frosting

Sweetened Whipped Cream

1 cup chilled whipping cream
1 to 2 tablespoons confectioners' sugar
1/2 teaspoon vanilla extract

In small mixer bowl combine cream, confectioners' sugar and vanilla; beat until stiff. Serve cold.

About 2 cups topping

Chocolate Whipped Cream

In small mixer bowl combine 1/2 cup sugar and 1/4 cup HERSHEY'S Cocoa. Add 1 cup chilled whipping cream and 1 teaspoon vanilla extract; beat until stiff. Serve cold.

About 2 cups topping

Quick Hot Fudge Sauce

2 tablespoons butter or margarine
1/3 cup HERSHEY'S Cocoa
1 can (14 ounces) sweetened condensed milk
2 tablespoons water
1 teaspoon vanilla extract

In heavy 2-quart saucepan combine all ingredients except vanilla. Cook over medium heat, stirring constantly with whisk, until sauce is smooth and slightly thickened, about 5 minutes. Remove from heat; stir in vanilla. Serve warm over ice cream or desserts.   *About 1 1/2 cups sauce*

Microwave Directions: In medium microwave-safe bowl place butter. Microwave at HIGH (100%) 30 to 45 seconds or until melted; stir in cocoa until smooth. Blend in sweetened condensed milk and water. Microwave at HIGH 1 minute; stir. Microwave at HIGH 1 to 2 additional minutes, stirring with whisk after each minute, or until mixture is smooth and warm. Stir in vanilla. Serve as directed.

Chocolate Peanut Butter Sauce

1/2 cup HERSHEY'S Chocolate Fudge Topping
1/2 cup HERSHEY'S Syrup
1/4 cup creamy peanut butter

In small saucepan place all ingredients. Cook over low heat, stirring constantly, until mixture is warm. Serve immediately over ice cream or other desserts.

About 1 1/4 cups sauce

Chocolate Sour Cream Frosting

1/2 cup butter or margarine
1/2 cup HERSHEY'S Cocoa
3 cups confectioners' sugar
1/2 cup dairy sour cream
2 teaspoons vanilla extract

In small saucepan over low heat melt butter. Add cocoa and stir constantly until mixture is smooth and slightly thickened. Transfer to small mixer bowl; cool slightly. Add confectioners' sugar alternately with sour cream; beat to spreading consistency. Stir in vanilla.

About 2 1/2 cups frosting

Cocoa Glaze

1 cup whipping cream
1 tablespoon light corn syrup
1 cup HERSHEY'S Cocoa
1 cup sugar
2 tablespoons butter or margarine
1 tablespoon vanilla extract

In heavy 2-quart saucepan stir together cream and corn syrup. Sift cocoa and sugar together; stir into cream mixture. Add butter. Cook over low heat, stirring constantly, 6 to 8 minutes or until butter melts and mixture is smooth; *do not boil.* Remove from heat; stir in vanilla. Use glaze while warm.

About 2 cups glaze

Note: Glaze can be stored in airtight container in refrigerator up to 2 weeks. Reheat over low heat, stirring constantly.

Fudgey Chocolate Fondue

1/2 cup butter or margarine
1/2 cup HERSHEY'S Cocoa
3/4 cup sugar
1/2 cup evaporated milk or light cream
1 teaspoon vanilla extract

In small saucepan over low heat melt butter. Remove from heat; immediately stir in cocoa. Add sugar and evaporated milk; cook over low heat, stirring constantly, until sugar is dissolved and mixture is smooth. Remove from heat; stir in vanilla. Serve warm with selection of fruit, marshmallows or small pieces of cake or cookies.

About 1 1/2 cups fondue

Fudgey Chocolate Fondue

Peanut Butter Sauce

    1 cup REESE'S Peanut Butter Chips
    1/3 cup milk
    1/4 cup whipping cream
    1/4 teaspoon vanilla extract

In small saucepan place peanut butter chips, milk and whipping cream. Cook over low heat, stirring constantly, until chips are melted and mixture is smooth. Remove from heat; stir in vanilla. Serve warm. Cover; refrigerate leftover sauce.

About 1 cup sauce

To reheat: Place sauce in small saucepan. Stir constantly over low heat until warm. Add additional milk or whipping cream for desired consistency.

Creamy Chocolate Frosting

    3 bars (3 ounces) HERSHEY'S
        Unsweetened Baking
        Chocolate
    1 cup miniature marshmallows
    1/2 cup butter or margarine,
        softened
    1/3 cup milk
    2 1/2 cups confectioners' sugar
    1/2 teaspoon vanilla extract

In top of double boiler over hot, not boiling, water melt baking chocolate. Add marshmallows; stir frequently until marshmallows are melted. Pour mixture into small mixer bowl. Beat in butter and milk until mixture is smooth. Add confectioners' sugar and vanilla; beat to desired consistency.

About 2 1/2 cups frosting

Easy Bittersweet Chocolate Sauce

    2 cups (12-ounce package)
        HERSHEY'S Semi-Sweet
        Chocolate Chips
    2 bars (2 ounces) HERSHEY'S
        Unsweetened Baking
        Chocolate, chopped
    1 cup whipping cream
    1 1/2 teaspoons vanilla extract

In top of double boiler over hot, not boiling, water place chocolate chips, baking chocolate and whipping cream. Cook, stirring frequently, until chocolate is melted and mixture is smooth. Remove from heat; stir in vanilla. Serve warm. Cover; refrigerate leftover sauce.

About 2 cups sauce

To reheat: Place sauce in small saucepan. Stir constantly over low heat until warm.

Chocolate and Vanilla Yule Log

    4 eggs, separated
    1/2 cup plus 1/3 cup sugar, divided
    1 teaspoon vanilla extract
    1/2 cup all-purpose flour
    1/4 cup HERSHEY'S Cocoa
    1/2 teaspoon baking powder
    1/4 teaspoon baking soda
    1/8 teaspoon salt
    1/3 cup water
        Vanilla Cream Filling (recipe
            follows)
        Chocolate Glaze (recipe
            follows)
        Vanilla Leaves (recipe follows)

Heat oven to 375°. Line 15 1/2 x 10 1/2 x 1-inch jelly roll pan with foil; generously grease foil. In large mixer bowl beat egg whites until soft peaks form; gradually add 1/2 cup sugar and beat until stiff peaks form. Set aside.

In small mixer bowl beat egg yolks and vanilla on high speed about 3 minutes; gradually add remaining ⅓ cup sugar. Continue beating 2 additional minutes until mixture is thick and lemon-colored. Combine flour, cocoa, baking powder, baking soda and salt; gently fold into egg yolk mixture alternately with water just until mixture is smooth. Gradually fold chocolate mixture into egg whites; spread batter evenly into prepared pan. Bake 12 to 15 minutes or until top springs back when touched lightly in center. Immediately loosen cake from edges of pan; invert onto linen towel sprinkled with confectioners' sugar. Carefully peel off foil. Immediately roll cake in towel starting from narrow end; place on wire rack. Cool completely. Prepare Vanilla Cream Filling. Unroll cake; remove towel. Spread with filling; reroll cake. Glaze with Chocolate Glaze. Cover; refrigerate until just before serving. Garnish with Vanilla Leaves.

10 to 12 servings

Vanilla Cream Filling

½ teaspoon unflavored gelatin
1 tablespoon cold water
⅔ cup **HERSHEY'S** Vanilla Milk
Chips
¼ cup milk
1 teaspoon vanilla extract
1 cup chilled whipping cream

Microwave Directions: In small cup sprinkle gelatin over cold water; let stand several minutes to soften. In small microwave-safe bowl microwave vanilla chips and milk at HIGH (100%) 30 seconds to 1 minute, stirring vigorously after 30 seconds, until chips are melted when stirred. Add gelatin mixture and vanilla extract; stir until gelatin is dissolved. Cool to room temperature. In cold small mixer bowl beat whipping

cream until stiff; carefully fold into vanilla mixture. Chill 10 minutes or until filling begins to set.

About 3 cups filling

Chocolate Glaze

2 tablespoons butter or
margarine
2 tablespoons **HERSHEY'S** Cocoa
2 tablespoons water
1 cup confectioners' sugar
½ teaspoon vanilla extract

In small saucepan over low heat melt butter; add cocoa and water, stirring until smooth and slightly thickened. *Do not boil.* Remove from heat; cool slightly. Gradually blend in sugar and vanilla; beat with wire whisk until smooth and slightly thickened.   *About ¾ cup glaze*

Vanilla Leaves

Non-toxic leaves (rose or
lemon leaves)
½ cup **HERSHEY'S** Vanilla Milk
Chips
1 teaspoon shortening

Microwave Directions: Thoroughly wash and dry several leaves. In small microwave-safe bowl microwave vanilla chips and shortening at HIGH (100%) 30 seconds to 1 minute, stirring vigorously after 30 seconds, until chips are melted when stirred. With small, soft-bristled pastry brush, brush melted vanilla mixture onto backs of leaves; place on wax paper. Refrigerate until very firm. Carefully peel green leaves from vanilla leaves; refrigerate until ready to use.

Cranberry Orange Ricotta Cheese Brownies

Filling (recipe follows)
1/2 cup butter or margarine, melted
3/4 cup sugar
1 teaspoon vanilla extract
2 eggs
3/4 cup all-purpose flour
1/2 cup HERSHEY'S Cocoa
1/2 teaspoon baking powder
1/2 teaspoon salt

Prepare Filling; set aside. Heat oven to 350°. Grease 9-inch square baking pan. In small bowl combine melted butter, sugar and vanilla; add eggs, beating well. Combine flour, cocoa, baking powder and salt; add to butter mixture, mixing thoroughly. Spread half of chocolate batter in prepared pan. Spread Filling over top. Drop remaining chocolate batter by 1/2 teaspoonfuls onto cheese mixture. Bake 40 to 45 minutes or until wooden pick inserted in center comes out clean. Cool completely. Cut into squares. Store leftovers in refrigerator.

About 16 squares

Filling

1 cup ricotta cheese
3 tablespoons whole-berry cranberry sauce
1/4 cup sugar
1 egg
2 tablespoons cornstarch
1/4 to 1/2 teaspoon grated orange peel

In small mixer bowl beat ricotta cheese, cranberry sauce, sugar, egg and cornstarch until smooth. Stir in orange peel.

Chocolate Festival Cheesecake

Chocolate Crumb Crust (recipe follows)
3 packages (8 ounces each) cream cheese, softened
1 1/4 cups sugar
1/4 cup HERSHEY'S Cocoa
1/2 cup dairy sour cream
2 teaspoons vanilla extract
2 tablespoons all-purpose flour
3 eggs
Assorted fresh fruit, sliced (optional)
Sweetened whipped cream or whipped topping (optional)

Prepare Chocolate Crumb Crust; set aside. Heat oven to 450°. In large mixer bowl combine cream cheese, sugar, cocoa, sour cream and vanilla; beat on medium speed with electric mixer until smooth. Add flour and eggs; beat well. Pour into prepared crust. Bake 10 minutes. Without opening oven door, decrease temperature to 250°; continue baking 30 minutes. (Cheesecake may not appear set in middle.) Cool 30 minutes. Loosen cheesecake from rim of pan; cool to room temperature. Chill several hours or overnight; remove rim of pan. Garnish with sliced fruit and whipped cream, if desired.

10 to 12 servings

Chocolate Crumb Crust

1 1/4 cups vanilla wafer crumbs (about 30 wafers, crushed)
1/3 cup confectioners' sugar
1/3 cup HERSHEY'S Cocoa
1/4 cup butter or margarine, melted

Heat oven to 350°. In small bowl combine crumbs, sugar and cocoa; blend in melted butter. Press mixture onto bottom and 1/2 inch up side of 9-inch springform pan. Bake 8 to 10 minutes. Cool.

Rich Chocolate Mini-Cakes

2/3 cup all-purpose flour
1/2 cup sugar
3 tablespoons HERSHEY'S Cocoa
1/2 teaspoon baking powder
1/4 teaspoon baking soda
1/4 teaspoon salt
1/2 cup water
3 tablespoons vegetable oil
1 teaspoon vanilla extract
  Chocolate Glaze (recipe follows)
  Vanilla Drizzle (recipe follows)

Heat oven to 350°. Lightly grease 24 small muffin cups (1 3/4 inches in diameter). In medium bowl combine flour, sugar, cocoa, baking powder, baking soda and salt. Add water, oil and vanilla; stir or whisk until batter is smooth and blended. (Batter will be thin.) Spoon batter in prepared cups filling 2/3 full. Bake 12 to 14 minutes or until top springs back when touched lightly in center. Cool in pans on wire rack 3 minutes; invert onto rack. Cool completely. Prepare Chocolate Glaze; dip rounded portion into glaze or spread glaze on tops. Place on wax-paper-covered tray; chill 10 minutes to set glaze. Prepare Vanilla Drizzle; drizzle onto mini-cakes. Decorate as desired.
About 2 dozen mini-cakes

Chocolate Glaze

2 tablespoons butter or margarine
2 tablespoons HERSHEY'S Cocoa
2 tablespoons water
1 cup confectioners' sugar
1/2 teaspoon vanilla extract

In small saucepan over low heat melt butter; add cocoa and water, stirring until smooth and slightly thickened. *Do not boil.* Remove from heat; cool slightly. Gradually blend in sugar and vanilla; beat with wire whisk until smooth and slightly thickened.   *About 3/4 cup glaze*

Vanilla Drizzle

1/2 cup HERSHEY'S Vanilla Milk Chips
1 tablespoon shortening

Microwave Directions: In small microwave-safe bowl microwave vanilla chips and shortening at HIGH (100%) 30 seconds; stir until smooth. If necessary, microwave at HIGH additional 15 seconds or just until chips are melted and smooth when stirred.

Milk Chocolate Pots de Creme

2 cups (11.5-oz. package) HERSHEY'S Milk Chocolate Chips
1/2 cup light cream
1/2 teaspoon vanilla extract
  Sweetened whipped cream (page 88) or whipped topping (optional)

In medium microwave-safe bowl place milk chocolate chips and light cream. Microwave at HIGH (100%) 1 1/2 minutes; stir. If necessary, microwave at HIGH an additional 15 seconds at a time, stirring after each heating, until chocolate is melted and mixture is smooth when stirred. Stir in vanilla. Pour into demitasse cups or very small souffle dishes. Cover; refrigerate until firm. Serve cold with sweetened whipped cream, if desired.   *6 to 8 servings*

INDEX